A Guide to the Common Birds of Cape Cod

by Peter Trull

Illustrated by Kathy Clark

Cape Cod Museum of Natural History

Acknowledgments

This book would not have been possible without the help of several folks. I wish to thank Beth Lehr for that phone call saying, ''Peter, write this book!'' and Mike O'Connor, owner of the Bird Watcher's General Store in Orleans, for his generosity in making it all possible. John Hay and Jonnie Fisk contributed to this project in several ways, and I thank Robert Cousins and Greg O'Brien for their early advice. Peter Trimble, Sally Clifton and Blair Nikula read the manuscript and made suggestions that improved the text; for this I am grateful. I also wish to thank Nancy Phinney for her editing skills, Kathy Schrock for her help on the computer and a special thank you to the real Elizabeth Taylor for her many hours of transferring the finished manuscript to computer, then dealing with my changes and additions over and over and over. Thanks to Lee Roscoe for the use of her ''What is Where When'' concept creating the ''Total Fieldmark'' format, used in the field walks section of this book.
. . . Finally I wish to thank Joanne Corsano and Gillian Drake for their help in bringing the manuscript to its finished form, the CCMNH Publications Committee for their help throughout the process, especially Robert Finch for advice, Arne Manos for seeing things through, and Susan Lindquist for her patience.

In Memoriam

Arne Manos

Cover illustration by Carol Dennis Trull

Printed on 100% recycled paper

Printed and designed by
Shank Painter Printing Company Inc.,
Provincetown, MA

Dedication

This book is dedicated to E. Vern Laux, Jr., whose personality and expertise got me fired up fifteen years ago and the enthusiasm appears permanent;
Richard A. Forster, whose expertise, patience and guidance took me through ten of the best years of my life working with terns;
Dr. Ian Nisbet, who changed my life and taught me things about birds I could never have learned elsewhere.

Contents

Introduction

Seven hundred species are too many to sort through when birding on Cape Cod. For instance, when a small, white, heron-like bird is observed in a salt marsh in July, the novice opens a field guide and must identify this bird from one of as many as five species. This book quickly identifies the bird as a Snowy Egret and tells you why.

A Guide to the Common Birds of Cape Cod focuses on birds of the Cape and Islands that you *will* see, without confusing you with numerous choices. It tells you what species you are looking at and omits all the unlikely possibilities. Although it does not include every bird to be found on the Cape, this book does describe birds regularly seen at various times of the year. In a few cases uncommon birds are mentioned. It teaches people how to sort out the common birds according to their behavior, habitat, location, and season. It will be useful for anyone who needs a guide to birds throughout southern New England.

With six scenarios in the Birding Tour Sections, the reader is guided through a variety of habitats during each season on the Cape. You are shown what birds are common at a particular time and place. The illustrations are simple and diagnostic.

Identifying birds can be made easier if you focus on a few key points. First and foremost, use your binoculars to find the birds. Scan the horizon, the marshes, and tidal flats continually. When trying to locate a bird in a tree, orient yourself by using its trunk, a branch, or a fork; then look for the bird. Once you have found the birds you can get down to the fun of identifying them. Here are a few pointers to make identification easier.

1. **Judge the size.** Is the bird sparrow, robin, or crow-sized? It may be smaller or larger.

2. **Determine what type of bird it is.** Is it a perching bird such as a robin? Or is it a heron? A duck? A hawk? A shorebird? What features are distinctive: the head, beak, back, wings, or legs?

3. **Judge the overall color pattern.** Many birds may be sorted out by the face pattern. Warblers and ducks, for example, have distinctive face patterns. Also, look for wing bars on small perching birds.

4. **Think about the location of the bird.** Is it on the ground? In the water? In a tree top?

5. **Think about what the bird is doing.** Is it flying close to the water? Soaring overhead? Hovering? Remember when identifying feeding shorebirds that a sandpiper probes while walking, whereas a plover stops, pecks, runs, and stops and pecks again.

6. **Refer to a field guide.** Several available field guides provide color illustrations or photographs of birds found in regional areas of North America.

One of the most popular guides is the first volume of the Peterson series, *A Field Guide to the Eastern Birds.* Over 500 species are represented with illustrations and range maps. Author Roger Tory Peterson teaches his invaluable field mark system for field identification. Another popular guide is a book in the Golden

Guide series, *Birds of North America.* This guide describes 700 species of breeding birds, migrants, and casual visitors found in North America. Range maps and color illustrations assist in the identification of common and not-so-common birds.

The National Geographic *Field Guide to the Birds of North America* is excellent for the experienced birder, with over 800 species described.

A field guide with photographs, the *National Audubon Society Guide to North American Birds* groups birds by shape and color rather than by taxonomic order. This system is often confusing for the beginner. For example, males and females of the Common Eider are shown several pages apart. This guide could serve, though, as a supplementary reference to the others mentioned. Any of the above guides would supplement this Cape Cod guide nicely. Most importantly, take your time and enjoy the birds. Think the opposite of confusion. Sort them out. Take your time and have fun. Bird watching is a no-pressure hobby for beginners, casual birders, or families on a drive with binoculars in the car.

Map of Cape Cod

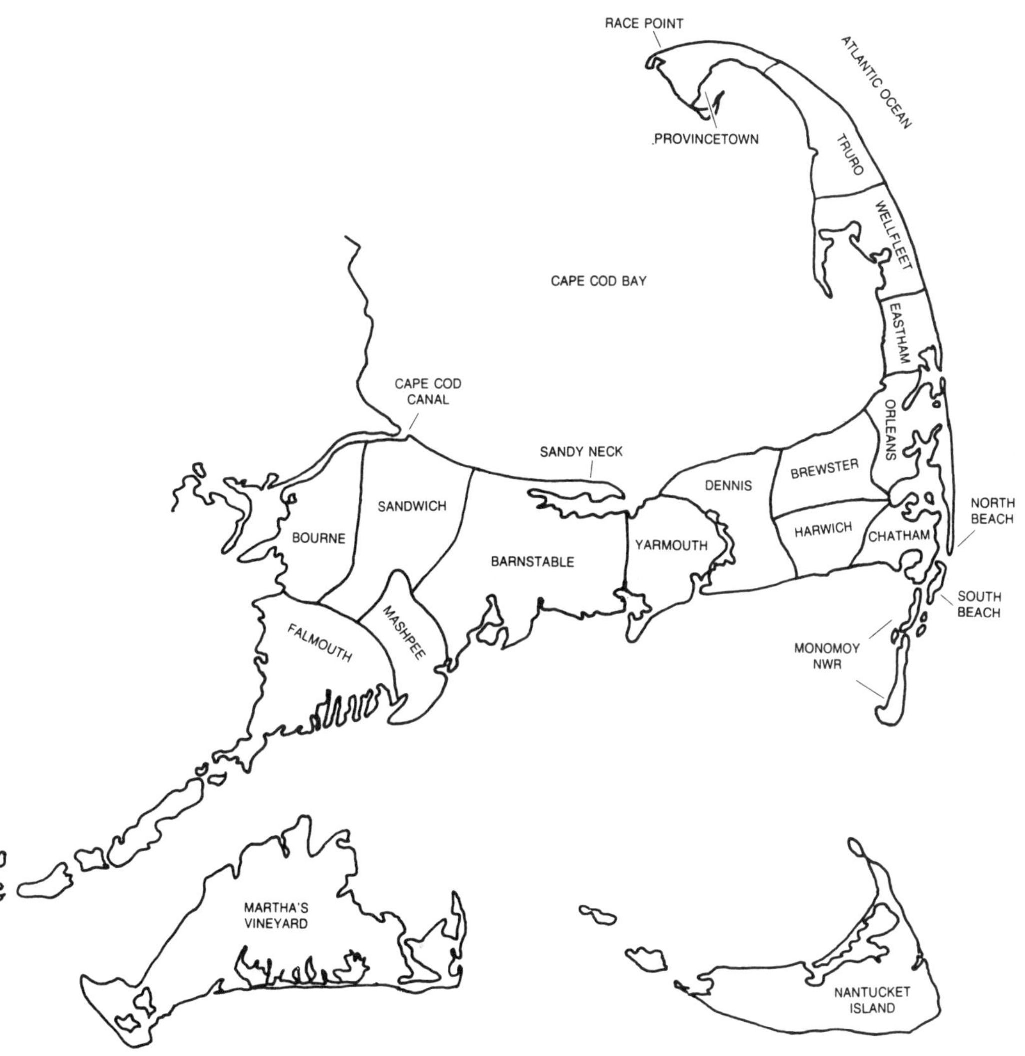

Parts of a Bird

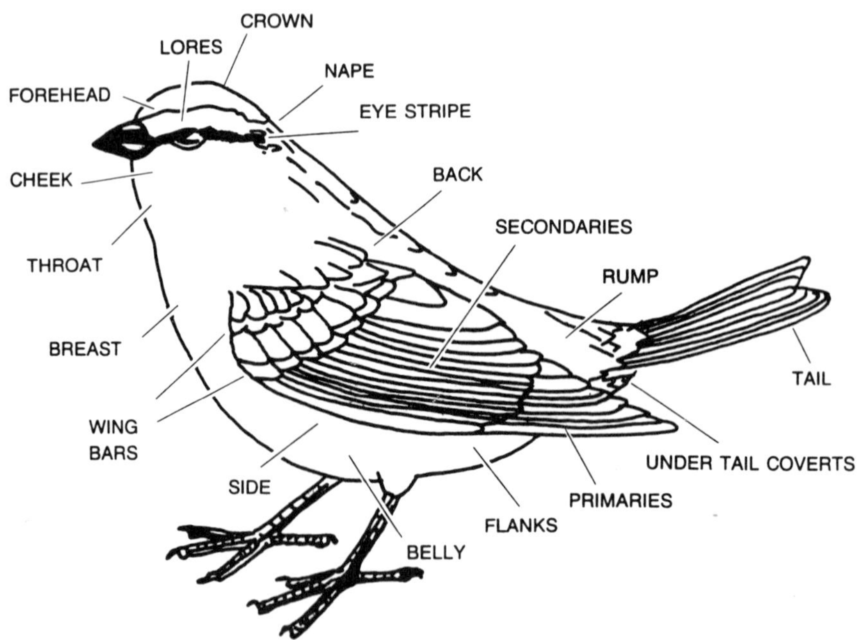

Accounts of Individual Species

Loons & Grebes

On Cape Cod, we see two species of loons and three species of grebes. The Common Loon, Horned Grebe, and Pied-billed Grebe are seen easily in certain habitats. The Red-necked Grebe and Red-throated Loon are less common and appear in habitats similar to those of the Common Loon and Horned Grebe, in the open waters of Cape Cod Bay, Nantucket Sound, and the Atlantic Ocean. Loons and grebes differ from ducks in their plumage pattern. Primarily seen in non-breeding plumage, loons and grebes are dark birds with white chin, cheeks, and throat. Their beaks are more pointed than that of ducks. The exception is the Pied-billed Grebe, a freshwater or saltmarsh creek grebe, that is small, stocky, and brown overall in appearance. Observe persistently, for loons and grebes are deep divers and may remain submerged for a minute or more.

Common Loon 28-36'' (Sept.-May)

Found on large bodies of water, mostly open ocean. A large ducklike bird with a daggerlike bill. Seen most often in non-breeding plumage. Common Loons appear dark, sometimes speckled, on the back with a white cheek, throat, and breast. They are usually solitary, but may appear in twos and threes.

Red-throated Loon 25'' (Oct.-May)

Seen in non-breeding plumage on the open ocean, mostly along the outer beach from Provincetown to Chatham, and in Cape Cod Bay. Smaller than the Common Loon. Same basic color pattern as Common Loon, but paler gray above. Bill appears to angle slightly upward and is thinner than Common Loon's. A grayer, smaller loon with a thin, upturned bill.

Horned Grebe 12-15 (Sept.-May)

Seen on open ocean in non-breeding plumage. Dark gray above with white cheeks and throat. Small, dark, pointed bill. As with all loons and grebes, the Horned Grebe occurs singly or in small groups.

Pied-billed Grebe 13'' (spring & fall)

Found on freshwater ponds and lakes. Small brown bird with pointed chickenlike bill. Bird in breeding plumage has dark ring on bill and black throat.

Shearwaters and Storm-Petrels

These birds are true seabirds and are seen primarily from boats. On whale watches, two species of shearwater, the Greater and Sooty, are very commonly seen. A third species, the Manx, is uncommon and a fourth, the Cory's, is rare. Storm-petrels are very small (smaller than a robin) and appear all black with a white rump. A relative of the shearwater, the Northern Fulmar is rare, but may be seen in the early spring or fall. Shearwaters, unlike gulls, soar close to the water's surface on narrow, stiff wings and often rise off the surface of the swells. Shearwaters and storm-petrels will follow boats if chum or food scraps are thrown overboard.

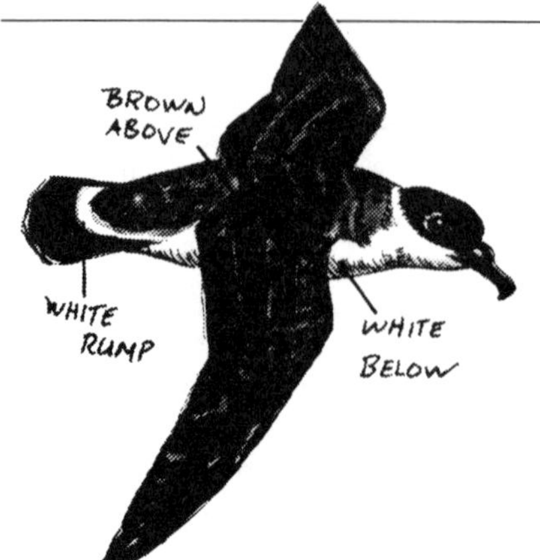

Greater Shearwater 19'' (May-Oct.)

A bird of the open seas and offshore waters. Observed near shore when blown in by nor'easters, storms with northeast winds. Dark brown above, pale underneath with a white rump patch. Dark brown cap and a pale collar around the neck.

Sooty Shearwater 17'' (May-Oct.)

Frequently seen on summer whale watches. Any all-dark, chocolate brown shearwater is the Sooty Shearwater. Quite unmistakable. Underwings (almost silvery) appear paler than the rest of the plumage.

Wilson's Storm-Petrel

7'' (May-Oct.)

Rarely observed except at sea. Considered the most numerous seabird. A wandering, open ocean species. Cardinal-sized. All black with white rump; faint, whitish diagonal bar across each wing. This storm-petrel often follows boats and patters over the surface with legs dangling.

Gannets

Northern Gannet 38'' (Oct.-May)

A very large white seabird with black wing-tips. Appears pointed on four sides: at each wing, the beak, and the tail. Dives beak-first from high above water. Often seen in large numbers. Easy to identify because of large size. Seen from the shore in Cape Cod Bay and from Provincetown to Chatham. Immatures are the same size and shape as adults and may be either solid brown or blotchy brown and white.

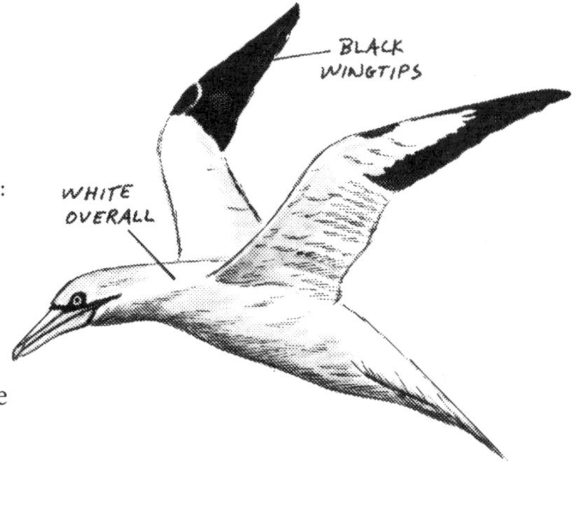

Cormorants

Cormorants are tall, upright standing, black birds, which occur singly or in groups. Unlike most other birds, they lack the oil gland that is used to oil their feathers to waterproof them. Cormorants therefore become watersoaked when they dive. Hence, the pose of cormorants standing with wings open, drying in the sun, is typical. Two species of cormorants occur on Cape Cod. One species is observed primarily in summer, the other in winter. There is little seasonal overlap.

Double-crested Cormorant

33'' (April–Nov.)

Seen over the entire Cape, often standing on docks or pilings with wings spread or flying overhead in flocks. Larger than a gull, all-black with orange throat patch. Immatures are brown with white throat and breast. Cormorants appear to tilt head upward when swimming. This is the black, upright standing bird of summer.

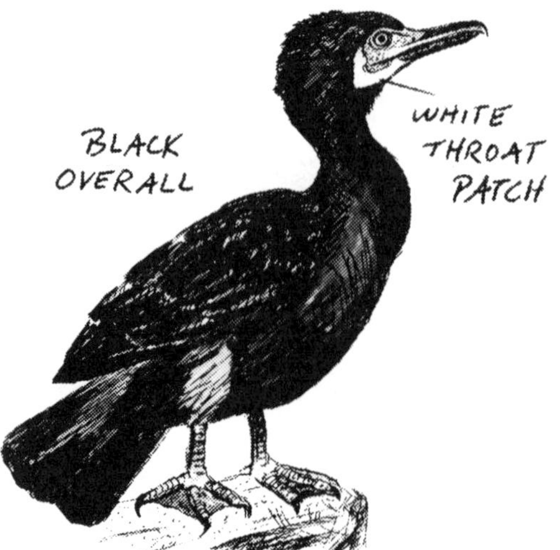

Great Cormorant

37'' (Oct.–April)

This large cormorant is the winter replacement of the Double-crested Cormorant. Shape and habits are similar. Large, all-black with small, yellow face patch bordered by a patch of white. Immatures are dark brown with pale throat and whitish belly. Remember, a general rule of thumb is: Double-crested Cormorant occurs in summer; and Great Cormorant, in winter. There is little seasonal overlap.

Herons and Egrets

Herons are long-legged, mostly long-necked, wading birds of the fresh- and saltwater shorelines. The herons and egrets most often seen on Cape Cod are the Snowy Egret, Great Blue Heron, Black-crowned Night Heron, and Green-backed Heron. The American Bittern is rare, as is the Great Egret, an all-white heron which is almost as large as the Great Blue Heron. The Yellow-crowned Night Heron, Cattle Egret, Tri-colored Heron and Little Blue Heron are very rare.

Snowy Egret

20-27'' (April—Oct.)

This is the white egret we see in summer along marsh edges and shorelines. All-white with black beak, black legs, and yellow feet.

Great Blue Heron

42-52'' (August—May)

Like most herons, feeds alone, but roosts in groups. Tall (3-4 feet), bluish gray, with a pale face and yellowish beak. This is *the* big gray heron of winter. In flight, legs extend beyond body.

Black-crowned Night Heron

23-28'' (year round, more common May—Oct.)

Often seen roosting in trees. Boldly patterned gray, black and white. Black cap, back, and bill. Gray neck and wings. White throat, breast and belly. Immatures are brown and streaked. Ninety-nine plus percent of brown streaked herons are immature Black-crowned Night Herons. Black-crowns fly overhead at dusk calling a throaty *kwok*.

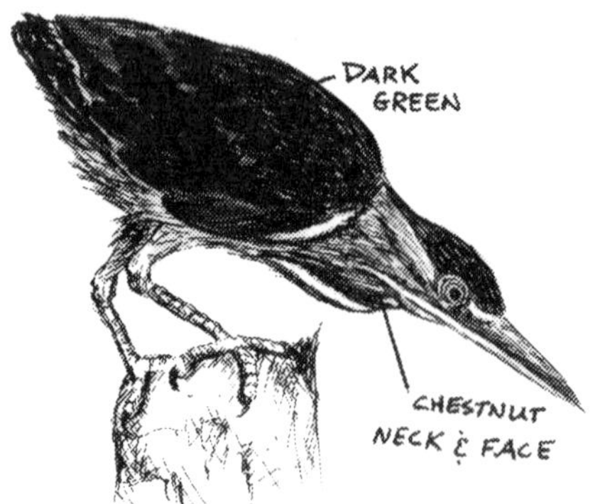

Green-backed Heron

(previously called Green Heron)

16-22'' (May—Sept.)

Solitary, nests in trees. Small, crow-sized. Dark green with chestnut neck and face, yellow legs, and bill. Most often seen perched motionless at water's edge. Call is a sharp *kyew.*

Swans and Geese

Mute Swan 60'' (year round)

An introduced species from Europe. Unmistakable, large and all-white, orange bill with a black knob at the base of bill. The only swan you are likely to see on Cape Cod.

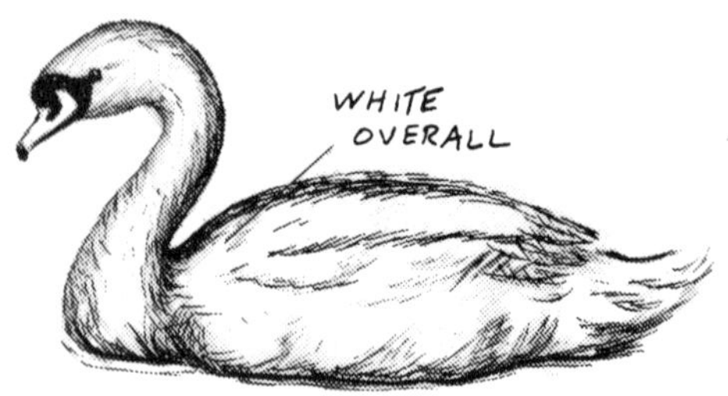

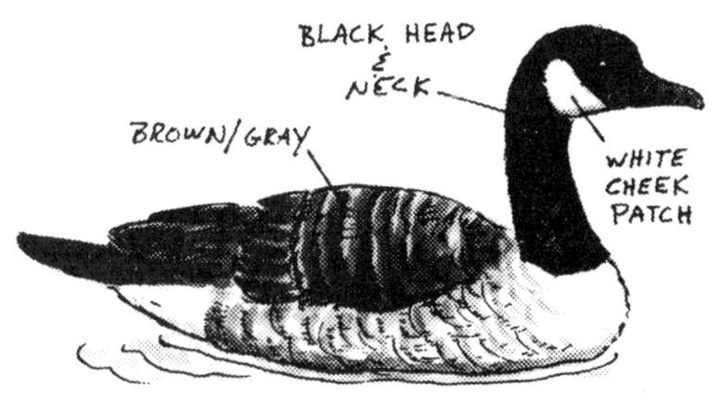

Canada Goose

25-43" (year round)

Needs little description. Common and widespread. Black head and neck, white bar on chin. Brownish gray on back with pale underparts. Shows white band on rump in flight.

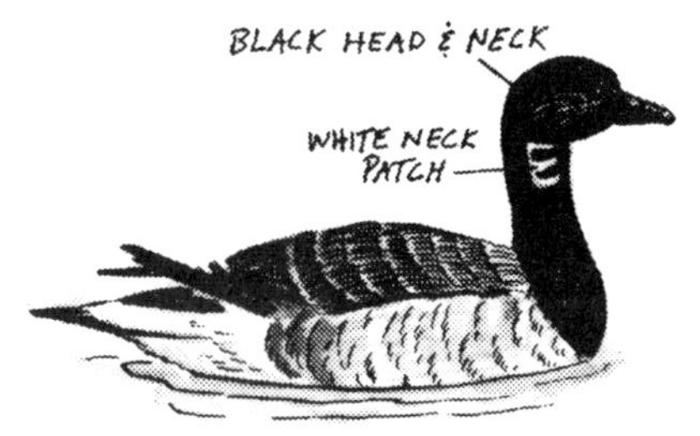

Brant

22-26" (Oct.–May)

A small, dark saltwater goose. Black head, neck, and breast. Dark brown back with white visible on the tail and a faint white mark on sides of the upper neck.

Ducks

Ducks are grouped by behavioral characteristics related to feeding habits. Dabbling ducks tip up to feed, with their tail up and head submerged to feed on submerged vegetation in shallow water. Dabblers spring from the surface to become airborne. Diving ducks use large, webbed feet for swimming underwater and use short, pointed wings for steering as they chase fish or feed on bottom plants. Diving ducks must run across the water's surface and flap to become airborne.

Diving ducks occur on both freshwater ponds and saltwater bays and may be observed in the company of dabbling ducks. Some females are difficult to identify from a distance, but males are easy to sort out with the help of a few simple markings.

Some diving ducks—the scoters, Common Eider, Common Goldeneye, and Bufflehead—are most often associated with saltwater bays and open ocean. A genus, or subgroup, of diving ducks, scoters are represented by three different species. All three scoters can be seen in Cape Cod Bay, off the Outer Cape, and in Nantucket Sound, often in large rafts.

Dabbling Ducks

Mallard 20-28" (year round)

The very common, green-headed duck. Male has white neck ring and rusty breast. Speculum is blue with white edges. Female is blotchy brown with dusky orange bill.

American Black Duck

21-25'' (year round)

In winter, the Black Duck is found in salt water along the shore, often in flocks. Both sexes are dark brown with paler brown head. Mustard yellow bill. Speculum is purple with no white edges.

Northern Pintail

26-30'' (year round, most often seen Sept.–April)

A distinctive brown, white, and gray duck. Male has brown head with white slash extending up from white neck. Back and sides gray. Long pintail is black and acute. Female is mottled brown with black bill. Notice *long* neck in both sexes. Not widespread on the Cape. In winter, look at Hallets Mill Pond off Route 6A in Cummaquid, Barnstable.

American Wigeon

18-23'' (year round, most often seen Sept.–April)

Gray face, white forehead and crown, and green patch through the eye set this handsome duck apart from others. Female head is plain gray. Both sexes have light, rusty brown breast and sides. Often seen in mixed flocks with other dabblers.

Green-winged Teal

14'' (year round, most often seen March-April and Sept.-Nov.)

A very small duck. When a flock of dabblers is observed overhead, teal are half the size of the others. Male has chestnut head with green patch through eye. Female is small and brown with small bill and green speculum.

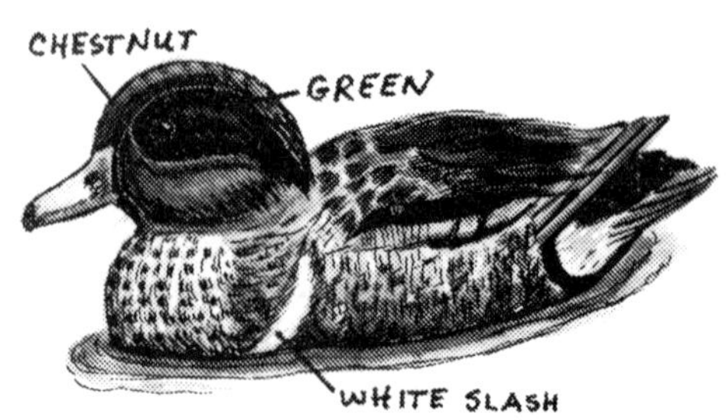

Blue-winged Teal

15-16'' (April–Oct., uncommon)

Male has gray head with distinctive white crescent on face in front of eye. A very small duck. Female is brown overall and difficult to distinguish from Green-winged Teal. Both sexes have a relatively large bill and powder blue speculum.

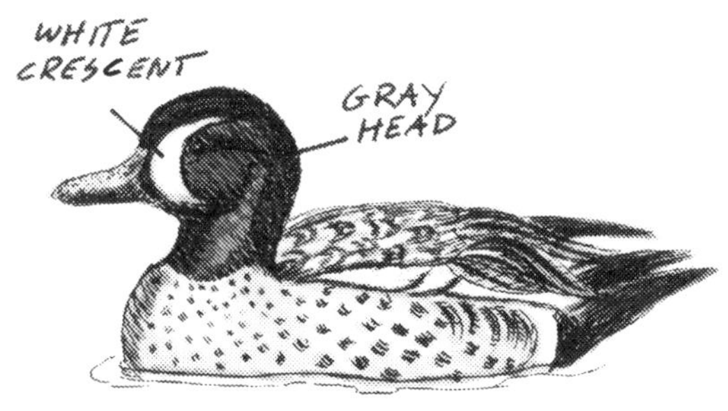

Diving Ducks

Ring-necked Duck

15-18'' (Oct.–April)

Black and gray. Black head, chest, and back; gray sides. *Note* white slash between dark chest and gray sides. This field mark will signify the male ring-neck at a distance. Both sexes have a white ring on bill. Female is brown with faint white eye-ring. Found on lakes and ponds.

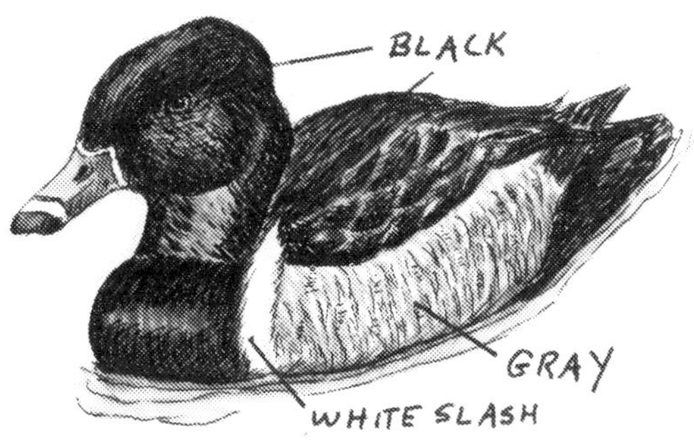

Greater Scaup

16-20'' (Oct.–April)

Similar to Ring-necked Duck, but no contrasting white slash on sides and no white ring on bill; gray back. Female scaups have a white patch around the base of the bill on the face. Seen on bays and lakes. A few Lesser Scaup also occur but are scarce and very difficult to separate from the Greater Scaup.

Canvasback

20-24'' (Nov.–March)

Uncommon, but often occur in large flocks when observed. A longish duck with a sloping head and long bill. Chestnut head, black breast, black tail, pale gray sides and back. Female is similar to male but duller overall. Seen on fresh-water ponds and in tidal rivers and bays.

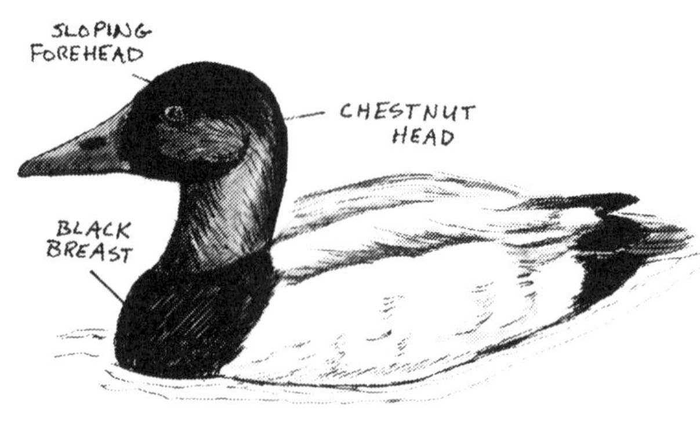

Common Eider 23-27''

(Sept.–May; a few present all summer)

A large black-and-white duck with a distinctive pattern. Male has a tinge of yellow green on the nape. Both sexes have a long, sloping forehead. Female is a rich, barred chestnut and dark brown. Often seen on open ocean in rafts of hundreds or thousands, especially in Cape Cod Bay and off the outer Cape.

Black Scoter 19''

(Oct.–April)

A stocky *all-black* duck with a distinctive orange knob at base of bill. Male shows *no white* anywhere. Female is brown with pale cheeks and throat.

White-winged Scoter

21'' (Oct.–April)

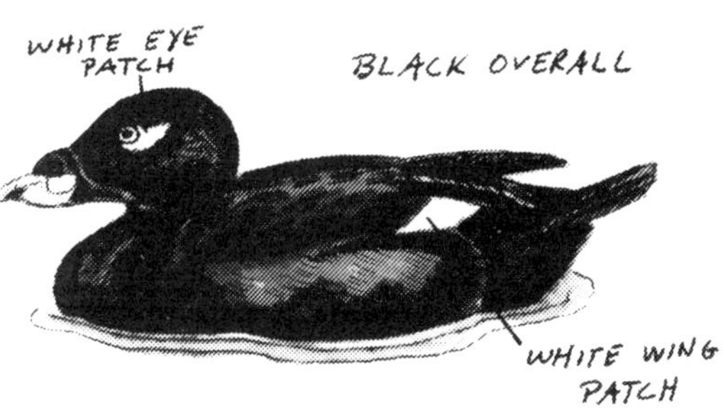

Black overall with a white comma over the eye and small white patch (not always visible) on the side (wing). In flight, it is the only *all-black* duck with large *white* patches on the rear of the wing. Female is brown overall; may also show the white patch on wing when swimming and has two pale patches on cheeks.

Surf Scoter 19'' (Oct.–April)

Black overall with a black, orange, and white bill. White patch on forehead and nape, thus its nickname skunkhead. Female is similar to female White-winged Scoter, but has no wing patch.

Common Goldeneye

18'' (Nov.–March)

Dark head with round white patch between eye and beak. White breast and sides. Dark back with white streaks on upper back. Female is grayish with brown head and whitish ring on neck; bays and large lakes.

Bufflehead 13-15'' (Nov.–April)

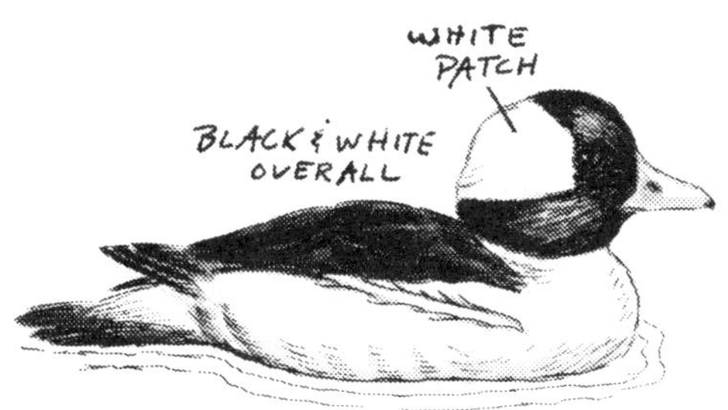

A very small, chunky black-and-white duck. Very common and widespread on both fresh- and salt-water. Male has a big white patch on rear of glossy, black head. Back is black; breast and sides, white. Female is dark brown with a white patch on cheek *behind* the eye.

Mergansers

Mergansers are fast-flying, fish-eating ducks. Beaks are thin and have serrated upper and lower mandibles. The Red-breasted Merganser is one of the most common saltwater ducks. Often thousands can be seen in a day.

Red-breasted Merganser

20-26'' (Oct.–May)

Observed most often on saltwater in two plumages. Adult males show dark green head and crest, white neck ring, gray, black, and white sides. Females and immatures brownish overall, with a rusty brown crest, head, and neck. Notice long neck and white wing patches as this bird flies fast over water.

Common Merganser

22-27'' (Nov.–March)

Found on lakes and ponds, this large, white-sided, green-headed bird has a bright red beak and no crest. Female is large and rusty brown overall.

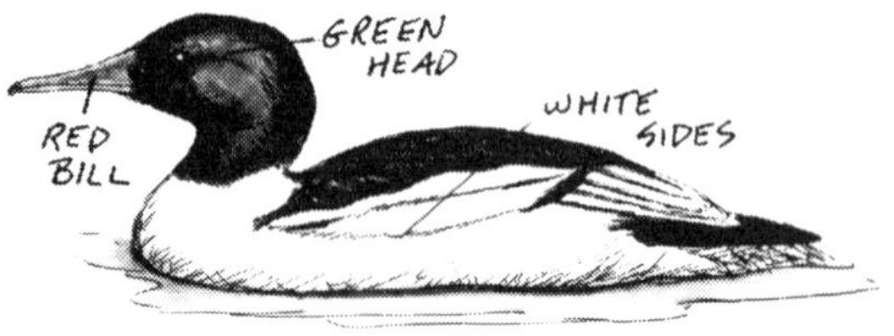

Hooded Merganser

16-19'' (Oct.–April)

Uncommon: found in ponds or brackish water. Male has striking, rounded, white crest, fringed by black; black neck and black-and-white breast. This bird's mohawk of black and white should help to identify it. Females are also crested, but brown overall.

Hawks, Ospreys, and Vultures

Raptors occur in good numbers on the Cape, both as migrants and nesters. Vultures are the least common of birds mentioned here, but should be easy to identify.

Hawks are generally separated into three groups which describe their overall shape and behavior.

Buteos are the soaring hawks, often observed circling overhead on broad wings, with tails fanned. Included in the Buteo group are the Broad-winged Hawk and Red-tailed Hawk.

Accipiters are the fast-flying, bird-eating woodland hawks. Accipiters have short, rounded wings and a long tail which aid in maneuverability through woods and thickets. Typical flight consists of several flaps; then a glide; then flapping and gliding repeatedly. This flight pattern is easily observed during spring and fall migrations. Accipiters include the Sharp-shinned Hawk, Cooper's Hawk and Goshawk.

Falcons are swift, powerful hawks, with **pointed wings** and a long tail. Falcons feed primarily on small birds. Our smallest falcon is the Kestrel, which hovers when hunting. Other falcons include the Merlin and Peregrine.

Turkey Vulture 26-32''

(March–Sept.)

Large, dark, soaring bird with two-toned, light-gray/dark-gray underwings. When soaring, Turkey Vultures hold their wings in a shallow V, and teeter or seesaw with the wind. Often seen soaring over highways.

Sharp-shinned Hawk

10-14'' (Sept.–May)

A small, bluejay-sized, bird-eating hawk. Long tail and short, rounded wings identify this, the **only** small hawk with **unpointed** wings. Appears brownish gray overall. Most often seen in flight which characteristically consists of several flaps, then a glide. This is the small hawk that terrorizes bird feeders.

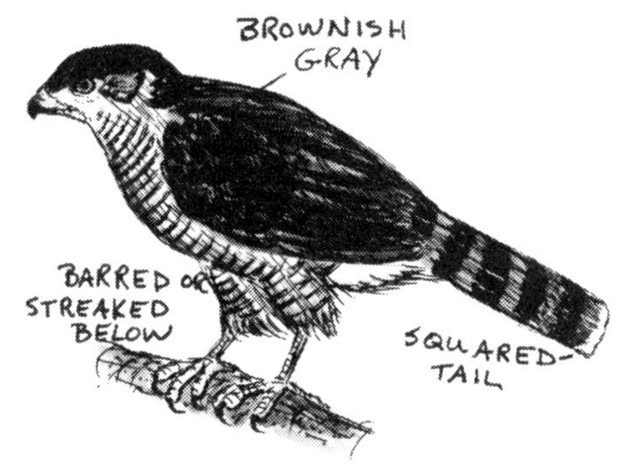

Red-tailed Hawk

19-25'' (year round)

A large, soaring hawk. Broad wings; very white underparts with a dark belly band and fanned, red tail are obvious as this bird soars overhead. Our commonest large hawk; often seen along the highway. Immature's tail is plain and brown instead of red.

Broad-winged Hawk

14-19'' (April–Sept.)

Crow-sized. Our only other common, broad-winged, fan-tailed, soaring hawk. Overhead, distinguished from red-tail by smaller size and wide, black-and-white bands on tail: look for these two field marks first. Immatures are brownish with narrower, paler tail bands. Often seen in numbers during spring migrations, particularly over the Outer Cape.

Northern Harrier

(formerly called Marsh Hawk)

17-24'' (year round)

This long-winged, long-tailed hawk is often seen flying low over salt marshes and dunes. A white rump patch seals the identification of this fairly common hawk. The harrier holds its wings in a shallow V in flight. Most harriers are brown females and immatures; the gray males are uncommon.

Osprey

21-25'' (March–Oct.)

A large, distinct, sharply contrasting dark-brown-and-white fish hawk. Often seen flying fairly high overhead. In flight, Ospreys show a distinctive crook, or bend, in the wings.

American Kestrel

9-12'' (year round)

Smallest North American falcon. Dove-sized. Long tail and *pointed* wings. Males are steel blue on upper wings; females have brown upper wings and back (mantle). A true wire bird, kestrels often perch on overhead wires along roadways and watch the ground below for mice and insects. Kestrels hover when hunting.

Pheasant, Grouse and Bobwhite

Of the Ring-necked Pheasant, Ruffed Grouse, and the Northern Bobwhite, only the Bobwhite needs to be mentioned in detail. The Ring-necked Pheasant male is brilliantly colored, large, and long-tailed. Although duller than the male, the female is also large and long-tailed. The Ruffed Grouse is brown, chunky, and crow-sized. Grouse may be seen streaking across the road or exploding into flight from the woodland floor in a roar of wings. Behavior and habitat of the Ruffed Grouse most often help to identify it.

Northern Bobwhite

8-11'' (year round)

A small chunky quail, often seen at feeders or crossing roads. Plumage is mottled reddish brown and white. Throat and the line through the eye are white. Our only small, quail-like bird. Often seen in groups (coveys) during fall and winter. Call is a ringing *bob-white.*

Rails

Three species of rails occur on Cape Cod. All are secretive and rarely seen. Clapper Rails are found in salt marshes. Virginia Rails and Soras are found in freshwater wetlands. Rails are distinctively shaped, chickenlike birds, most often heard at dawn or dusk. Clapper and Virginia Rail calls consist of the repeated single notes *kak, kak, kak, kak, kak* and *kik-kik, kik-kik, kik-kik* respectively. Soras give a shrill *whinny* or sharp single whistle. The secretive nature of rails allows few observations by the casual bird-watcher.

Shorebirds: Oystercatchers, Plovers, and Sandpipers

Shorebirds represent the birds of the tidal flats and shore edges. Knowing the common plovers and sandpipers of Cape Cod is the key to learning any uncommon and rare visitors. Of the fifteen species mentioned here, two-thirds are likely to be observed in large flocks ranging from twenty to several hundred birds. Remember, plovers locate food visually—they walk or run, stop, peck, run again, stop, and peck. Sandpipers use their tactile sense to locate food and so they probe **and** feed as they walk. Knowing these two types of behavior helps to narrow your choices in identifying a shorebird.

American Oystercatcher

17-21'' (April—Oct.)

Unmistakable! A large black, brown, and white bird of the tidal flats. Large, bright orange bill; yellow eye with orange eye-ring; pink legs. Found on mussel flats, particularly on Morris Island, Chatham.

Semipalmated Plover

6-8'' (May and July—Oct.)

Our only small, ring-necked plover of the tidal flats that is dark brown above and white below. One dark ring around the neck and a white forehead patch help to identify this small plover.

Piping Plover

6-8'' (March–Sept.)

Uncommon, but worth mentioning as these small sand-colored plovers nest and may be seen at several public beaches. Similar in size and appearance to Semipalmated Plover, but the piper is tan above, white below, with a single, dark, but often incomplete, neck ring.

Killdeer

9-11'' (March–Nov.)

Not easy to find on Cape Cod, this is the ring-necked plover of upland areas. Robin-sized with two dark neck rings. The killdeer is dark brown above, white below, and shows a rusty rump patch in flight. Found in pastures and open areas; nests on gravelly soil. Loud call is *kill-dee, kill-dee* or *dee-dee-dee.*

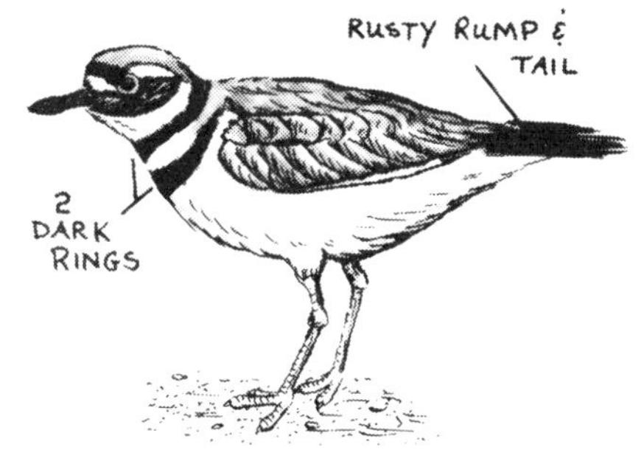

Black-bellied Plover

10-14'' (year round; most common April–May and July–Oct.)

The largest plover in North America. Males are unmistakable with a black face, throat, breast, and belly. Young or molting males may be blotchy black. A bright white stripe extends from the crown, down the sides of the neck, to the sides of the breast. Back is mottled black and white. Females, juveniles, and winter males look like a completely different bird: mottled grayish brown above and whitish below. Often seen in large flocks in high marshes during fall. All plumages show black axillars, or armpits, and an all-white tail in flight. This is our largest and most common plover.

Greater Yellowlegs

14'' (April–May and July–Nov.)

Medium-sized sandpiper with **bright yellow legs.** Blotchy, streaked, grayish brown and white overall. Often seen actively chasing small fish in shallow water. Call is a loud rapid three- or four-note *tew tew tew.*

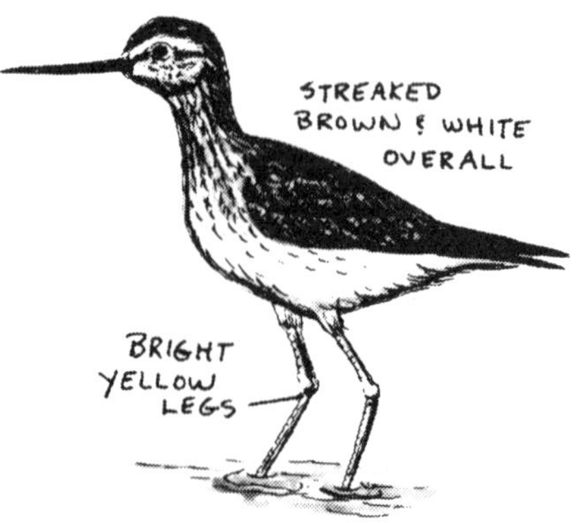

Willet

14-17'' (April–Sept.)

One of our largest sandpipers. Willets are grayish brown overall, with heavily barred breast and pale belly. Legs and beak are gray. Fairly nondescript when at rest, but in flight the Willet shows large, white wing patches. This bird nests on the Cape in salt marshes and is very noisy from June to August. Call is repeated *wi-wi-llet, wi-wi-llet, wi-wi-llet.*

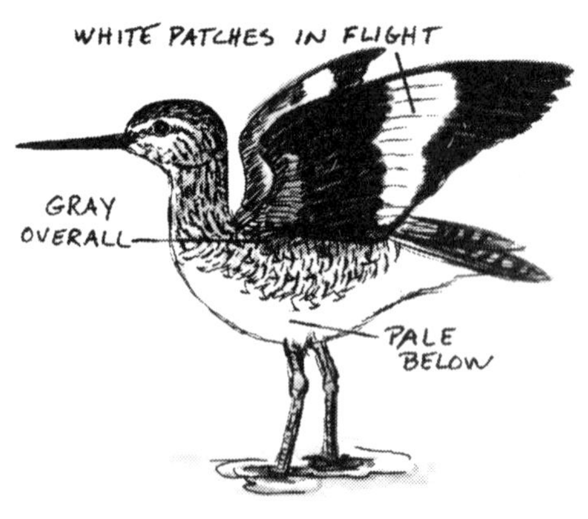

Whimbrel

15-19'' (July–Sept.)

Large and brown overall. Pale brown with streaks below and a striped crown of light and dark brown which shows a dark line through the eye. Most notable is the very long, decurved bill. Found in salt marshes where it feeds on fiddler crabs.

Ruddy Turnstone

8-10'' (May and July–Sept.)

The calico cat of the bird world. Unmistakable; rich chestnut, black, and white with orange legs. Flips stones, shells, seaweed with its bill in search of food on sand and tidal flats. Hence the name turnstone.

Red Knot

10-11'' (July–Sept.)

A medium-sized, chunky sandpiper with a relatively short bill. May be observed in two distinct plumages. Fall and winter birds are a nondescript grayish and white; breeding birds show a robin-red breast and belly. Birds in either plumage may appear together on tidal flats. Remember, **short** beak distinguishes knot from dowitcher which has similar plumage, but very **long** beak.

Sanderling

7-8'' (April–Nov., but may winter over)

Small, pale gray sandpiper. Some appear on the Cape in breeding plumage which is brick red on head, breast, and back. Belly is white. This is the bird that runs ahead of breaking waves on the outer beach. We see mostly the **pearl gray** non-breeding plumage.

Semipalmated Sandpiper

5-7'' (May and July—Sept.)

Small, very numerous sandpiper. Most often in large flocks on the tidal flats. Compare with tiny Least Sandpiper which prefers muddy tidal creeks and salt marshes. Semipalmated is **the** small, black-legged sandpiper of tidal flats. Somewhat nondescript; grayish brown above with pale breast and belly.

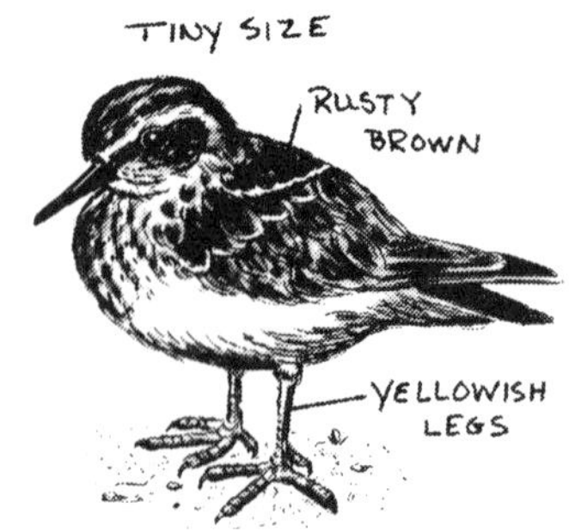

Least Sandpiper

5-7'' (April—May and July—Sept.)

Our smallest shorebird. Has **yellowish** legs and prefers salt marshes and muddy tidal creeks. Rusty brown on back and pale below. Any small sandpiper that flushes from a salt marsh is almost certainly a Least Sandpiper. Call is *breep, breep, breep.*

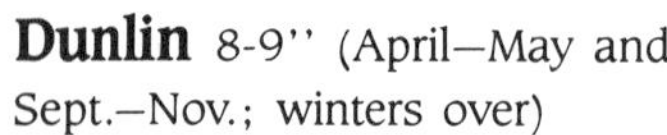

Dunlin 8-9'' (April—May and Sept.—Nov.; winters over)

Smallish, **long-billed** sandpiper which occurs in two plumages. In spring, the Dunlin shows a rusty back with a black belly smudge. Seen mostly in late fall in plain plumage of grayish brown and pale gray. Our latest arriving fall shorebird. Note relatively long bill on this small, grayish brown bird.

Short-billed Dowitcher

10-12'' (July—Sept.)

Dowitchers are medium-sized and chunky. Appears brownish red overall; easiest field mark is its **long, straight bill.** Also shows a pale eye stripe and, in flight, a white stripe up the middle of back.

Gulls and Terns

Gulls and terns are closely related species, gray above and pure white below, except the Great Black-backed Gull which is black above. These are birds of the seashore and open ocean, often observed foraging along beaches. Terns tend to be smaller and appear more streamlined than gulls. Terns can be separated from gulls by their small size and **black cap.**

Great Black-backed Gull

28-31'' (year round)

Our largest gull needs little description. White head, breast and belly; black back and wings. Takes four years to acquire adult plumage. Immatures appear mottled brown overall, with varying degrees of black on back, depending on age.

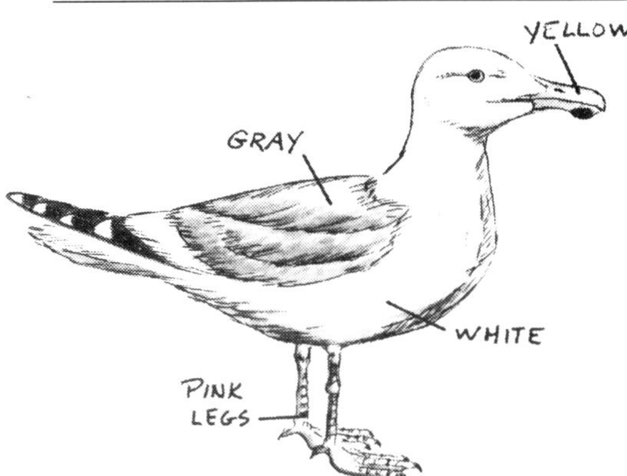

Herring Gull

23-26'' (year round)

The common ''sea gull'' with white head, breast, and belly and pale gray back and wings. Yellow bill with red spot near tip; pink legs. Takes four years to acquire adult plumage. Immatures appear mottled brown overall, with varying degrees of gray on back, depending on age.

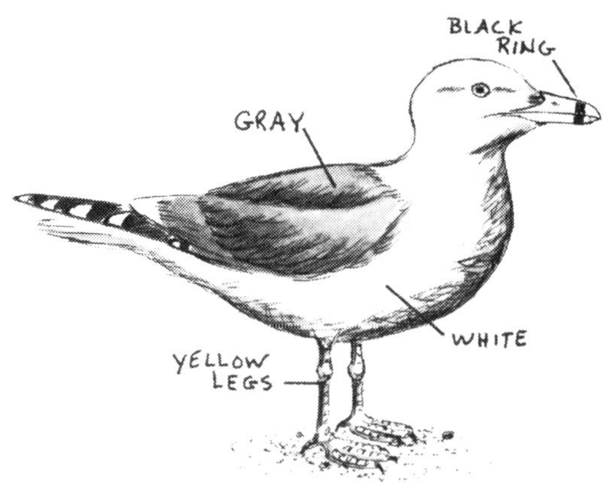

Ring-billed Gull 19'' (year round)

A small version of the Herring Gull, with two **main** differences. Adults have yellow bill with **black ring near tip** and **yellow legs,** rather than pink. Ringbills often flock in school yards, open fields, and parking lots. They nest around the Great Lakes and winter here, but some non-breeders are here in summer. Takes three years to mature. Immatures appear mottled brown overall, with varying degrees of gray on back, depending on age.

Laughing Gull

16-17'' (April–Oct.)

Our only common gull with a black head. Takes three years to mature. Immatures appear as a small, dusky grayish brown gull. Call is a loud *hah-hah-hah-haaaah* with variations. They nest on Monomoy Island and at New Island at Nauset Inlet, Orleans.

Black-legged Kittiwake

17'' (Sept.–April)

A small, gray-and-white winter gull of the open sea. Occasionally seen in **huge** numbers off the Outer Cape in winter. Two good field marks are its small, unmarked yellow bill and its **all-black** wing tips (they look as if they have been dipped in ink). Winter juveniles have a black bill and a distinct, black W pattern across wings which contrasts with a white wedge on rear of wings.

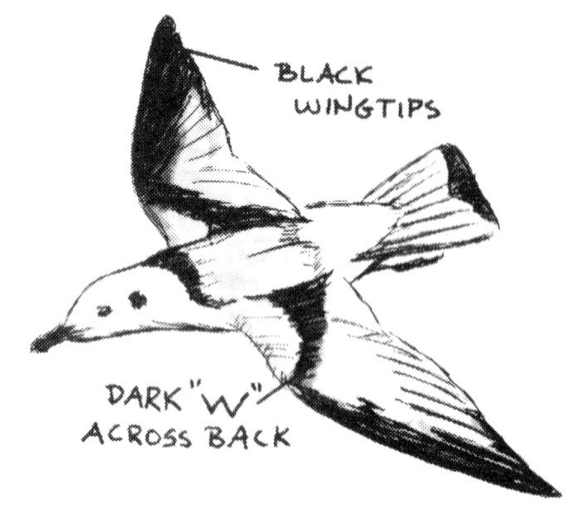

Common Tern

13-16'' (May–Oct.)

Most terns seen in summer are Common Terns. Gray above, white below; black cap, **orange** bill with a black tip, deeply forked tail. Call is a *kee-eer* or *kip-kip-kip.*

Roseate Tern

14-17'' (May–Sept.)

Uncommon but may be seen among flocks of Common Terns. Roseate Terns are **silvery white** with **black** bill and **long,** white, flowing tail feathers. **Listen** for call *chi-vik, chi-vik.*

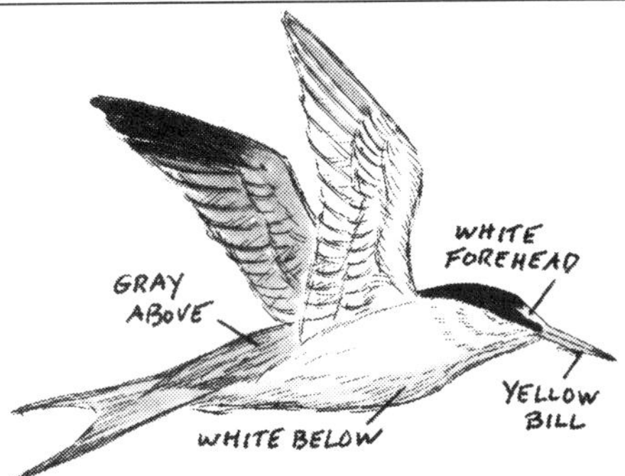

Least Tern 9'' (May–Aug.)

Our smallest tern. Gray above, white below, with a black cap and a **yellow** beak. Forehead is white. This delicate little tern is widespread, and may be seen diving for fish in fresh as well as salt water.

Doves and Pigeons

We have one dove and one pigeon on Cape Cod. Both are very common, but live very different lives.

Rock Dove 13'' (year round)

The basic pigeon; typically gray and iridescent, but hybrids range from multicolored gray, white, and black to all-white or -brown. Nests under highway bridges, on buildings, or church steeples.

Mourning Dove 12'' (year round)

A medium-sized, brownish gray dove with a long, pointed tail. Some iridescence and pinkish buff on the neck. Head appears relatively small. Often seen on wires and in areas with bird feeders. Inhabits open areas and fields.

Owls

There are two common owls on Cape Cod and they are both very widespread. The Great Horned Owl is big and eats whatever it wants. The Eastern Screech-Owl is small and lives in hollow trees. A third species, the Saw-whet Owl, is rare, secretive, and heard mostly in coniferous woodlands. The saw-whet call is a long series of toots, over and over.

Great Horned Owl

18-25'' (year round)

More often heard than seen. A very large owl with ear tufts and big, yellow eyes. Nests in large pines. Call of repeated, deep, loud hoots is heard most often during winter.

Eastern Screech-Owl

7-10'' (year round)

A small gray or reddish-brown owl with ear tufts. Screech Owls inhabit any area with large deciduous trees, particularly near water. From November to March Screech Owls may call anytime during evening hours, beginning just after dark and usually ending before dawn. Call is a soft, quavering trill or low, monotone, warbling whistle.

Swifts

Chimney Swift

5-6'' (May-August)

The Chimney Swift is only seen in flight and can be identified by its call alone—a constant twittering overhead, especially at dusk. A small, dark cigar with wings. Long wings and rapid wingbeats identify this, our only swift.

Kingfishers

Belted Kingfisher

13''(year round)

A medium-sized, crested bird. Solitary, often perches on overhead wires or pilings. Richly blue head, breast band, back, and wings; white breast and neck ring. Female has a second rusty band across belly. Feeds by hovering and diving for live fish. Found near ponds, bays, and estuaries. Our only kingfisher.

Woodpeckers

We have three common woodpeckers on Cape Cod: two look very similar, but are different sizes, and the third is a woodpecker that feeds mostly on the ground.

Downy Woodpecker

6-7'' (year round)

The small, black-and-white woodpecker of woodlands and suet feeders. Sparrow-sized. Male shows red on back of head. Note thin bill and black spots on white outer tail feathers.

Hairy Woodpecker

9-10'' (year round)

Less common than the Downy Woodpecker. Noticeably larger than downy, but nearly identical. Heavier bill than Downy Woodpecker and all-white outer tail feathers. Associated with extensive woodlands.

Northern Flicker

12-14'' (year round)

Robin-sized; often found on the ground where it feeds on ants. **White rump patch** immediately signifies the flicker in flight. Yellow under-wings, spotted breast and belly, and barred back all help in identification, but look for **white rump patch.** Male has red patch on back of head and black mustache on face.

Flycatchers

Three species of flycatchers are commonly seen on Cape Cod and all three nest here. These are small to medium-sized birds. All are 6-9 inches in length and can be separated easily for identification. Flycatchers habitually sit on a dead or exposed branch, flit out after an insect, and return to the same perch. Each of Cape Cod's common flycatchers has a distinct field mark that should help to identify it quickly. A fourth species of flycatcher, the Eastern Wood Pewee is an uncommon woodland nester. It is similar to the Eastern Phoebe but it has two wing bars. Its call is *pee-a-wee.*

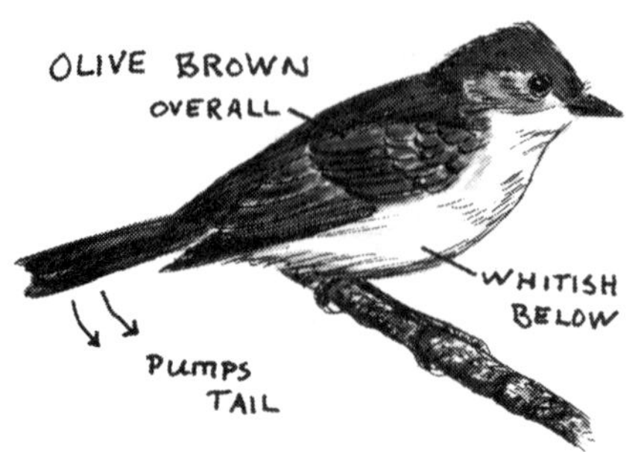

Eastern Phoebe

6-7'' (March-Oct.)

A bird that is almost always found near water. Olive brown above with whitish (yellowish in immatures) underparts; **no wing bars.** Song is buzzy *fee-bee.* Look for tail movement up and down when it is perched. Nests under shack or garage eaves and under bridges near streams.

Great Crested Flycatcher

8-9'' (May-Sept.)

A bird of the oak woodlands; easier to hear than see. Dark olive above, white throat, yellow breast and belly. Appears slightly crested. In flight, shows reddish flash in wings and tail. Listen for loud *wheep, wheep* call in tree tops.

Eastern Kingbird

8'' (May-Sept.)

Distinctly black above and pure white below. White band across end of tail. Often noisily twittering near pond edges. Occurs, more than other flycatchers, in open areas.

Lark

Only one species of lark is found on Cape Cod and it occurs year round both as a nester and winter resident. Found readily on beaches and dune areas.

Horned Lark

7-8'' (year round)

A ground-dwelling bird of open areas. Sometimes shows distinct, black horns against a face and throat of yellow; black eye patch. Brown on back with black breast patch and pale underparts. Depending on their sex and age, Horned Larks can be brightly and distinctly patterned or nondescript and brown. **Habitat** is a good clue to identification. Savannah Sparrows share the same habitat, but are heavily streaked and smaller. Listen for the Horned Lark's twinkly, metallic song on beaches. Often runs over dunes.

Swallows

Six species of swallows occur on the Cape, but only two are widespread and common. These are the Tree Swallow and Barn Swallow. The Northern Rough-winged Swallow is brown above and white below and nests in sandbanks and cliffs or under bridges. Bank Swallows are almost identical, but have a brown band across the chest. The Cliff Swallow and Purple Martin occur while on migration, do not nest here, and are very rare.

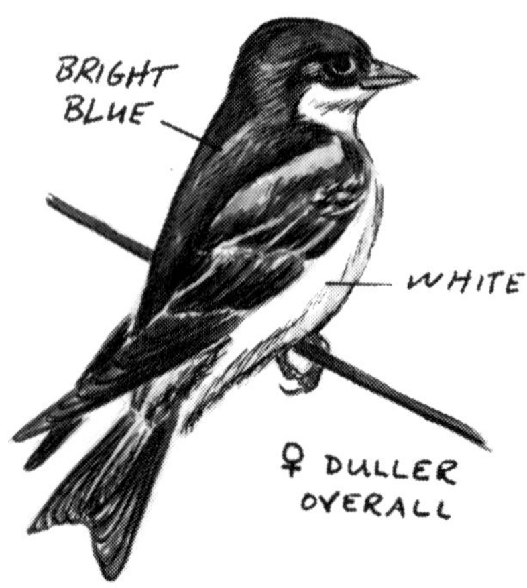

Tree Swallow

5-6'' (April-Oct., abundant in Sept. during fall migration)

Males are bright blue above, pure white below. Females are similar, but duller blue gray. The common swallow of nest boxes. Zigzags over open areas to catch insects in flight. Does not have a deeply forked tail like our other common swallow, the Barn Swallow. During September, Tree Swallows migrate by the thousands along the shores of Cape Cod, sometimes in seemingly endless flocks.

Barn Swallow

6-8'' (April-Sept.)

Dark, rich blue above, cinnamon buff below, with a reddish throat. Note the deeply forked tail. Zips through the air to catch insects on the wing. Makes a nest on barns, rafters, bridges; often nests in groups.

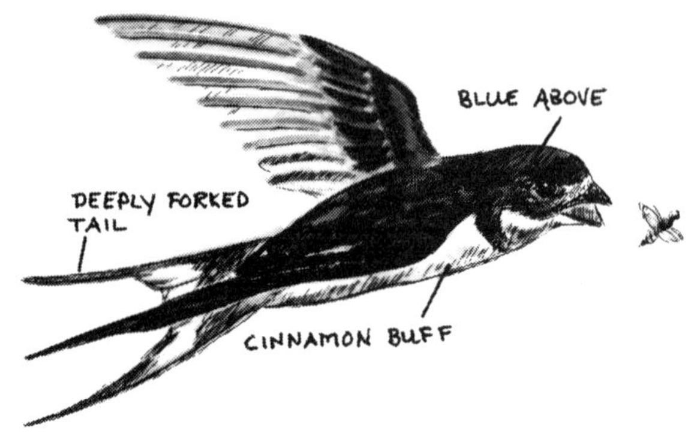

Jays and Crows

Neither jays nor crows need much description. We see but one species of each on Cape Cod. Both are rowdy, raucous, and intelligent.

Blue Jay

11-13'' (year round)

A bright blue, crested jay with a black necklace on white underparts. Blue Jays inhabit oak woods and visit feeders regularly.

American Crow

17-21'' (year round)

This is our roadside crow, larger than any other black bird we see on the Cape. All black, including legs and bill. Often in flocks; especially aggressive when harassing hawks or Great Horned Owls.

Chickadees and Titmice

Our familiarity with the Black-capped Chickadee is probably greater than with the Tufted Titmouse. However, both are very common and related to each other. Both titmice and chickadees occur at bird feeders and are at home in the Cape's oak woodlands. Often these tough little birds flock together in winter, when they actively move about in search of insect eggs and larvae.

Black-capped Chickadee

4-6'' (year round)

Very common and widespread. Small, gray above, buffy below with a black cap and bib. Call is a nasal *dee, dee, dee* or, in spring, a clear, two-note whistle.

Tufted Titmouse

6'' (year round)

Our **only** small gray-and-white, **crested** bird. Gray above, white and creamy buff below. Beady eyes and black patch on forehead. Call is a three or four note whistle, often given from treetops. Gives a nasal buzz when excited or alarmed.

Nuthatches

Two species of nuthatches occur on Cape Cod. Both are somewhat uncommon, but may occur regularly at feeding stations. Nuthatches habitually walk headfirst down tree trunks and over branches. One species prefers the oak woods; the other, pines.

White-breasted Nuthatch

5-6'' (year round)

White face, black cap, and grayish blue back and wings. White breast and belly with reddish flanks help to identify this acrobat of the oak woods and bird feeders. Slightly larger than a chickadee. Female has same pattern but is duller overall. Call is a nasal *ank, ank.*

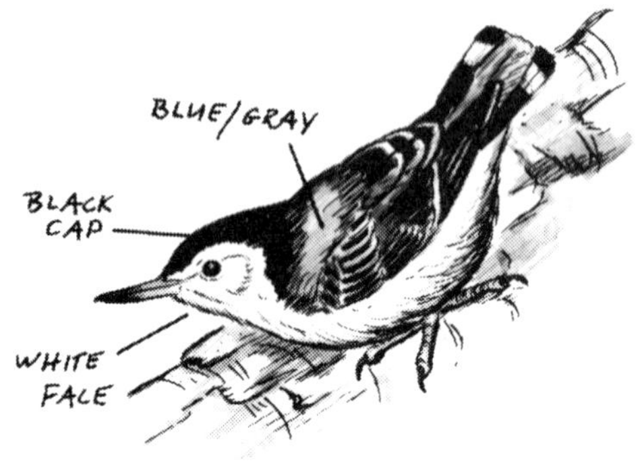

Red-breasted Nuthatch

4'' (Year round)

A bird of the pine woods; smaller than a chickadee. Rusty breast and belly, blue gray back, black cap, and black line through the eye against a white face. Female has same pattern but is duller overall. Also climbs headfirst down tree trunks. Fairly uncommon; numbers fluctuate year to year. Comes to feeders and beef suet.

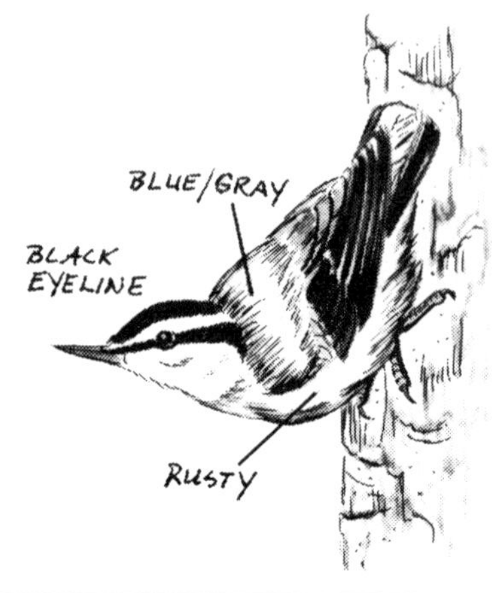

Kinglets and Gnatcatchers

These tiny woodland sprites are associated mainly with spring and fall warbler migrations. The Golden-crowned Kinglet winters on the Cape.

Ruby-crowned Kinglet

4'' (April-May and Sept.-Oct.)

Tiny, olive green above, whitish below. Never stands still, constantly fluttering wings. Often seen in numbers during spring migration. Look for two yellowish wing bars and a white eye-ring.

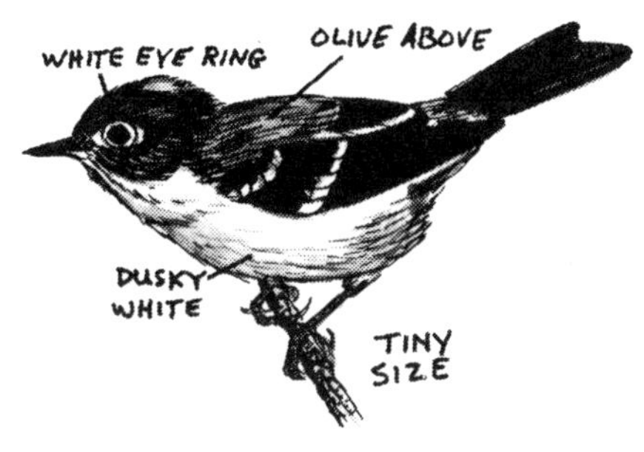

Golden-crowned Kinglet

3-4'' (Oct.-April)

Tiny, olive green above, whitish below, but most easily identified by bright yellow orange crown patch and a white line through the eye against a dark face. Prefers evergreens; often observed with roving flocks of chickadees and nut-hatches in winter.

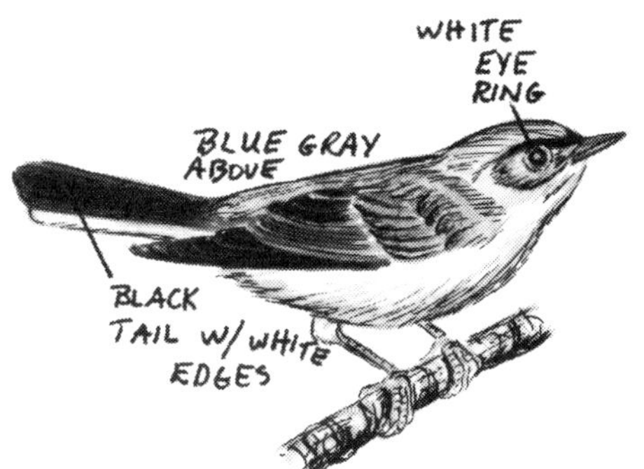

Blue-gray Gnatcatcher

4'' (April-May)

This tiny version of a mockingbird is seen mainly during spring migration. An active, long-tailed, gray-and-white bird with white outer tail feathers and a white eye-ring. Gray above, white below, with a black tail. Call is a nasal *speee.*

Thrushes

The American Robin is a true thrush and is very common and widespread. No other thrushes are common on Cape Cod. Only one is seen regularly during migration, Swainson's Thrush. The Wood Thrush, Hermit Thrush, and Veery do occur. Consult a field guide if your thrush is not a Swainson's.

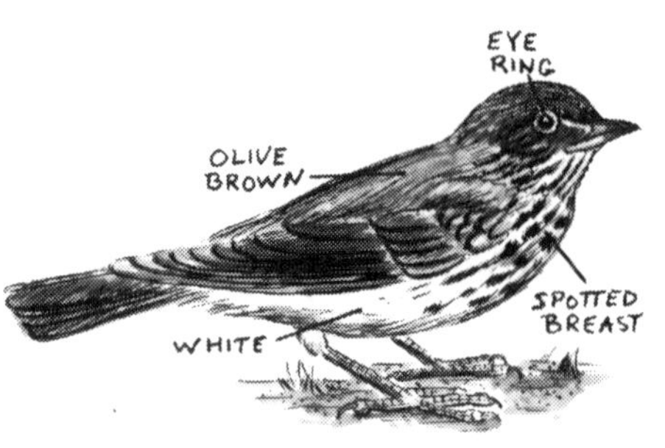

Swainson's Thrush

7'' (May and Sept-Oct.)

Separate this thrush from other possibilities by white or buffy eye-ring and buffy face and breast with dark breast spots. Clean, whitish belly. Wood Thrush has eye-ring, but has large spots on **entire breast** and **belly.** Hermit Thrush also has eye-ring, but has **very rusty** tail contrasting with olive brown back. Swainson's Thrush always has uniform, olive brown back and tail.

American Robin

9-11'' (March-Oct., but some may occur year round)

Dark gray back, darker head, rusty red breast. Seen on lawns, very widespread. Listen for song at dawn and dusk *cheeri-o, cheeri-o, cheeri-up.*

Mimic Thrushes

Three species of mimic thrushes occur on Cape Cod. The first, the Brown Thrasher, is less widespread and more secretive. The other two, the Gray Catbird and the Northern Mockingbird, are very common. All three mimic thrushes are excellent songsters. All like shrubs and thickets and have noticeably long tails.

Brown Thrasher

11-12'' (April-Oct.)

Looks like a cross between a thrush and a mockingbird. Rich, reddish brown above and heavily spotted below, but with a long tail. Adult Brown Thrasher has yellow eyes.

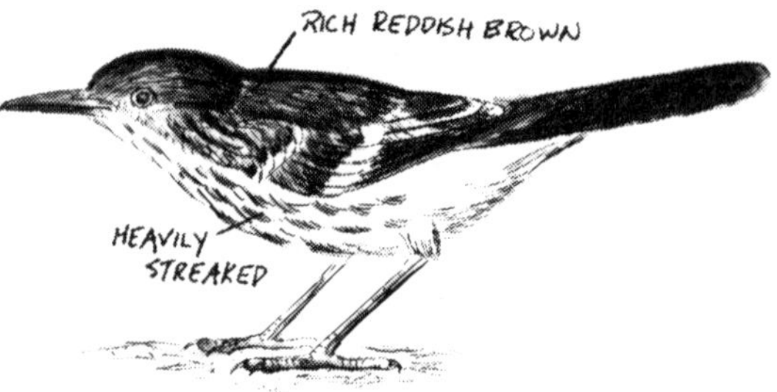

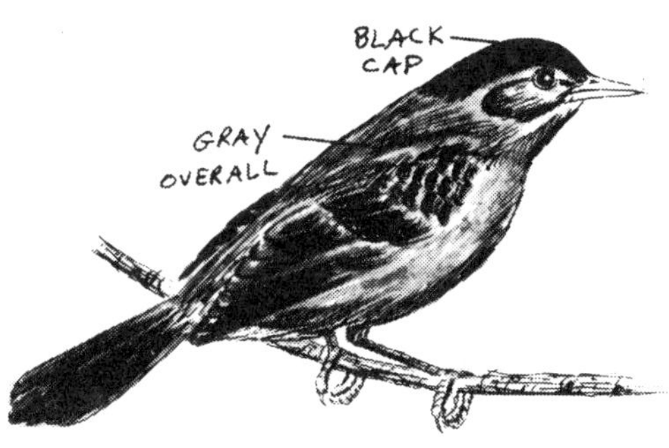

Gray Catbird

9'' (May-Oct.)

Dark gray overall with black cap, black tail, and chestnut brown undertail coverts. If you have shrubs and thickets in your yard, catbirds probably nest there. Song is a bubbly, squeaky, gurgling cacophony of notes; also makes a catlike meow.

Northern Mockingbird

9-11'' (year round)

A long-tailed, gray-and-white bird with large, white wing patches and white outer tail feathers. Gray above, darker tail and wings, white below. **An excellent mimic**, it imitates everything–from other birds and animals to music. Prefers multiflora rose and other thickets. May sing all night long.

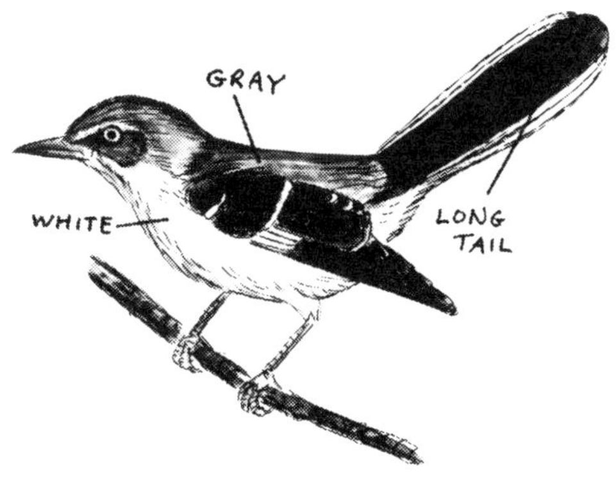

Starlings

The starling is an introduced species which has become abundant throughout all of the United States. They often outrival native species for nesting cavities.

European Starling

(year round)

A glossy black, short-tailed, black bird with yellow beak. Appears speckled during fall and winter. Often seen on wires or in treetops. Series of calls is a cacophony of squeaks, twitters, and chirps. Starlings form huge flocks in salt marshes during late summer and fall.

Vireos

Vireos are often associated with warblers, especially during spring and fall migrations. But, their bills are short and stout compared to the needle pointed, tweezerlike bill of warblers. Only the Red-eyed Vireo is common on the Cape, although the Solitary Vireo, with its bluish head, white spectacles, and white wing bars, occurs during migration.

Red-eyed Vireo 6'' (May-Sept.)

Drab olive green on the back, but with a gray cap and a white stripe above the eye bordered above and below with black. This vireo sings all day, all summer, from tree-tops in deciduous woods. Much more often heard than seen; usually three or four melodious phrases sounding somewhat robinlike.

Warblers

The very word warbler excites novice and expert birder alike. For many, spring warbler migration is **the** most exciting time of year. Although the fall plumage of warblers is known to be nondescript, some males may occur in full or partial breeding plumage during fall migration. All nineteen species mentioned here are common in breeding plumage during spring migration.

Warblers are tiny (chickadee-sized or smaller), brightly colored, fast-moving insect eaters. Their identification can be made easier by following a few basic steps. First, separate warblers by determining whether or not the species has **wing bars.** This will cut your choices by about fifty percent. Next, look on the breast for streaking or a **''necklace.''** This will limit your choices further. Third, look at the colors and pattern on the **face and head.** All warblers are distinctly different. Rather than seeing them as a confusing group, sort them out.

Wing Bars:

Northern Parula 4-5'' (May-Sept.)

A tiny, short-tailed, blue, yellow, and white warbler. Blue back, yellow throat, white belly. Two white wing bars. Male shows reddish and black across breast. Notice olive green patch on the back. Key your observation on blue, yellow, and white color pattern. Only two regularly occurring warblers have blue backs. The other is the Black-throated Blue Warbler. The Parula nests in a few spots on Cape Cod.

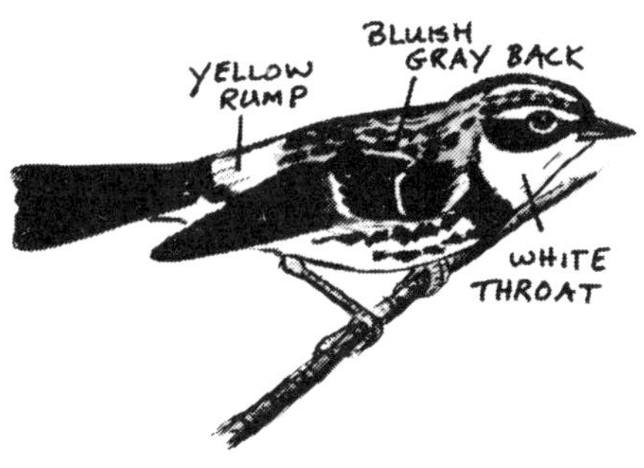

Yellow-rumped Warbler

5-6'' (Sept.-May)

Our only wintering warbler. The winter plumage is nondescript, brownish gray above and whitish below. **Bright yellow** rump in all birds. Breeding plumage is bluish gray, black, yellow, and white. Yellow rump, crown, and side patches; black face; white throat; bluish gray on back. White below with black across the breast. Often found in flocks among bayberry thickets on outer beaches during fall migration and winter.

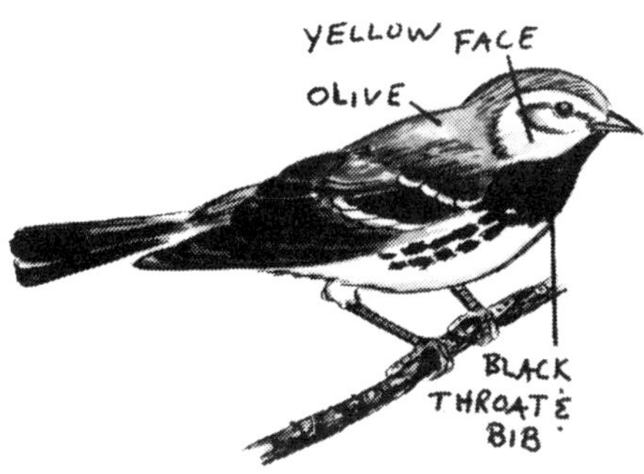

Black-throated Green Warbler

4-5'' (May and August-Sept.)

Should be called black-throated **yellow** warbler since its face, which contrasts with the black throat and bib, appears more yellow than green. Olive green on back; dark wings with white wing bars and white belly. Key on yellow face and black throat. Song is *zee-zee-zee-zoo-zee.*

Pine Warbler

5-6'' (April-Oct.)

A drab, yellowish treetop warbler. Pine Warblers nest in tall pitch pines throughout Cape Cod. We rarely see them in the dense canopy they occupy, but their monotone, yet musical, trill is heard often, especially in May and June. Dull yellow breast, white belly, and two white wing bars help to identify this warbler.

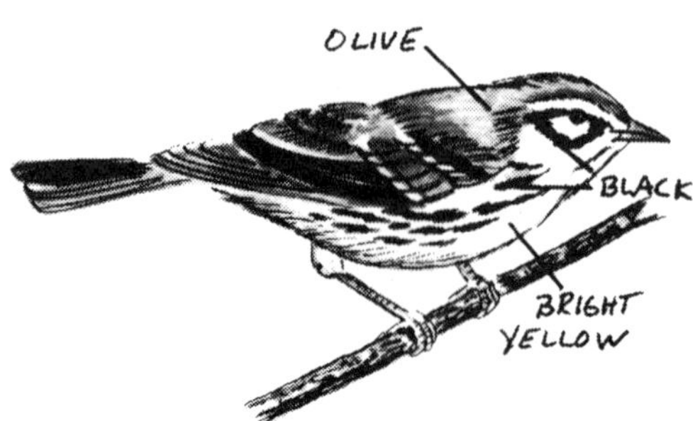

Prairie Warbler

5'' (May-Sept.)

A common nester of open scrublands and overgrown meadows. Also look along power lines where vegetation is low. Easy to identify by its distinctive song—a series of *zee* notes with a rising inflection. Prairie Warbler is olive on the back with yellow eyebrow, yellow patch below the eye, and bright yellow throat, breast, and belly. Shows black line through the eye and through the cheek; black specks on sides of body. Key on the song and a black-and-yellow face.

Black-and-white Warbler

5'' (May-Sept.)

Streaked black and white on face, throat, back, breast, and sides. Only the belly is pure white. Clings nuthatchlike to tree trunks and branches. Often seen in abundance during May. Song is a series of high, thin *wee-see, wee-see, wee-see, wee-see, wee-see.*

Magnolia Warbler

4-5'' (May and Sept.)

Black, yellow, and white. Look for black face, yellow throat, white eyebrow, white wing patch. Also yellow rump patch and white patches on tail. Breast is yellow with black streaks; belly is yellow. Focus on the black, yellow, and white color pattern.

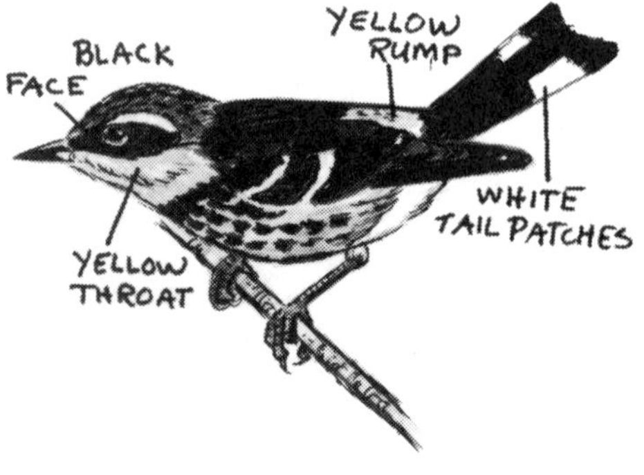

No Wing Bars:

Yellow Warbler

5'' (May-Sept.)

A common nester throughout the Cape, especially near water. Yellow overall, yellow olive on back. A short-tailed, yellow warbler we see all summer long. Male has red streaks on breast. Song is *sweet, sweet, sweet, sweeter than sweet.*

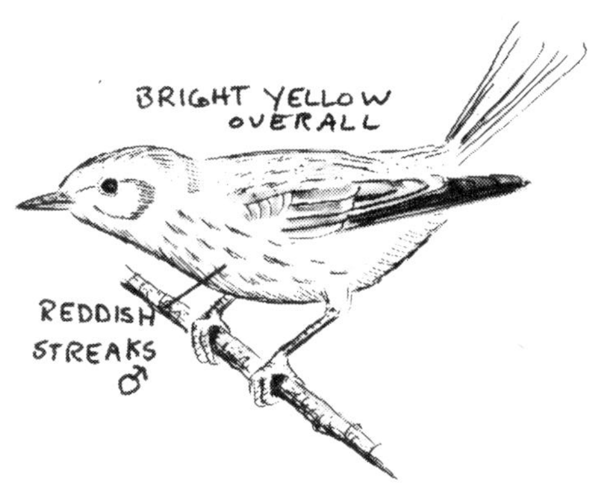

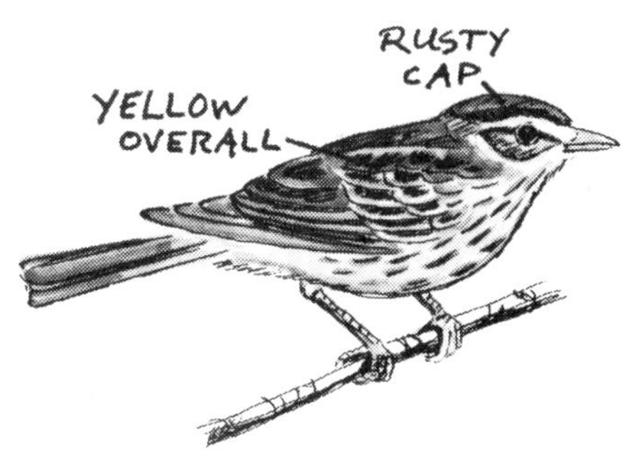

Palm Warbler

5'' (April-May; Sept.-Oct.)

A ground-dwelling warbler which appears yellow with a rusty cap in spring. In fall, drab olive overall with a **yellow rump.** This species wags or pumps its tail up and down **constantly**—a good identification clue. Palm Warbler is usually on or near the ground.

American Redstart

5'' (May-Sept.)

Male is an unmistakable, glossy black with orange patches in wings and tail. Female is similarly patterned but gray and dull yellow. Often flashes tail and wings while chasing insects. Like all warblers, the redstart is a tiny, fast-moving bird.

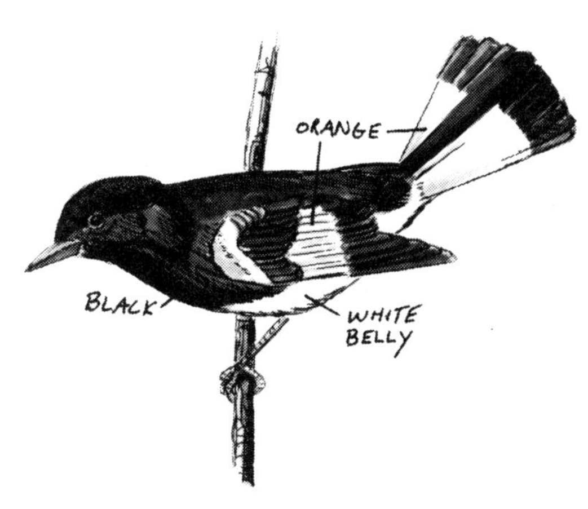

Common Yellowthroat

5'' (May-Oct.)

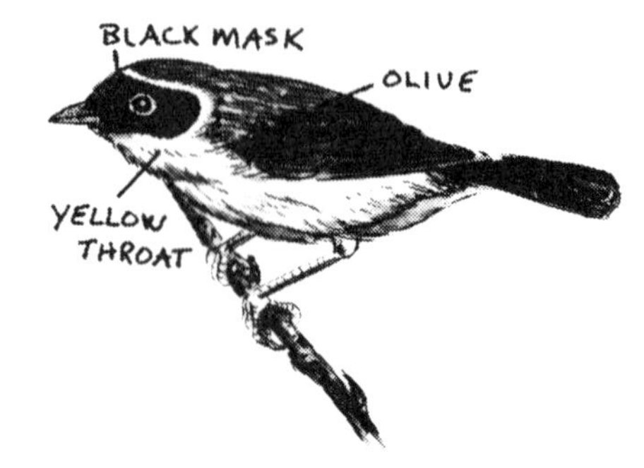

Olive on the back; bright yellow throat, breast, and belly. The male's banditlike mask helps to identify it immediately. Female is olive with bright yellow throat. Yellowthroats nest low in dense shrubbery.

Ovenbird 6'' (May-Aug.)

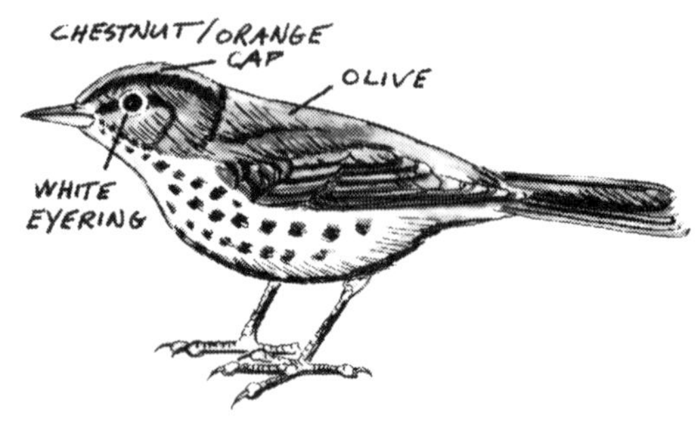

A small thrushlike warbler; lives on the ground and is more often heard than seen. Song is a loud, repetitive *teacher, teacher, teacher, teacher, teacher,* which starts softly and becomes steadily louder. Olive above with white eye-ring and chestnut orange cap. Pale below with brown streaking.

Other spring warblers that the casual birdwatcher may encounter are:

- **Chestnut-sided Warbler**
  5'' – Wing bars. Yellow cap; black line through eye; chestnut sides.

- **Cape May Warbler**
  5'' – White wing patch. Chestnut face patch bordered with yellow; yellow throat; breast and belly heavily streaked with black.

- **Black-throated Blue Warbler**
  5-6'' – White wing patch. Vivid blue back and wings; black face, throat, and sides; white belly.

- **Blackburnian Warbler**
  5'' – White wing patch. Fiery orange face with black eye patch; black back.

- **Blackpoll Warbler**
  5'' – White wing bars. Like Black-and-white Warbler except all white face and black cap.

- **Wilson's Warbler**
  5'' – No wing bars. Easy to identify—bright yellow underparts and face with black cap. Olive yellow back and wings.

- **Canada Warbler**
  5-6'' – No wing bars. A beautiful, gray-backed warbler with a yellow throat, breast, and belly. Note black necklace and white eye-ring.

Cardinals

Northern Cardinal

7-9'' (year round)

Everybody's favorite. All-red bird with crest. Male has a black face patch; female is a duller gray-green overall.

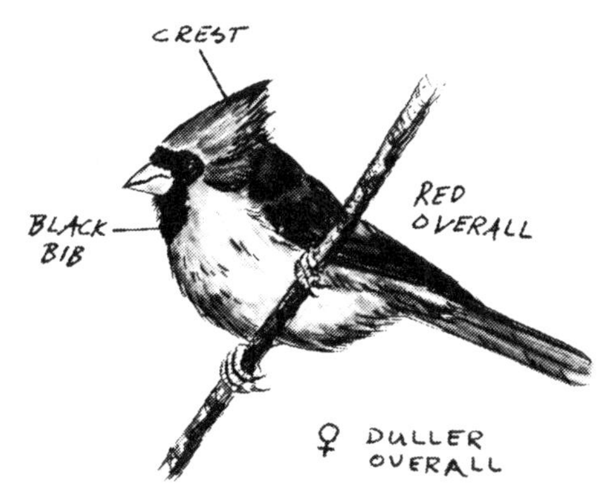

Towhees

Rufous-Sided Towhee

7-9'' (April-Oct.)

A secretive bird, whose call–*chew-wink* or *drink-your-teee*–is often heard before it is seen. Male is black on head, back, and throat; sides bright rufous; belly white. Female is brown on head, back, and throat. This is a bird of scrub-oak and pine woodlands.

Sparrows

Small, chiefly brown-and-white, ground-dwelling birds. Several show yellowish or buffy ochre highlights in plumage. Like the warblers, most of these are distinctly different in plumage patterns and habitat preference. So, when identifying sparrows, look at the habitat. Observe the sparrow's behavior–you will find some sparrows can be identified almost on the basis of behavior alone. When you note the field marks, look first at the breast to see if it is plain or streaked.

Chipping Sparrow

5'' (April-Oct.)

Clearly defined plumage; chestnut cap, white eye stripe with a black lower edge; clean, white throat, breast, and belly identify this small, long-tailed sparrow. Look for chippies around and under pitch pines.

Savannah Sparrow

4-6'' (April-Nov.; small numbers occur year round)

This is the small, streaked sparrow of the open, grassy **dunes** and meadows. Most sparrows seen in dune grass are savannahs. Shows pale yellow on face.

Sharp-tailed Sparrow

5-6'' (May-Oct.)

A small, **salt marsh** sparrow with buffy underparts, gray nape, ochre face, and short tail. This is **the** sparrow of the salt marsh. Virtually any sparrow in the wetter areas of the salt marsh is a sharp-tailed.

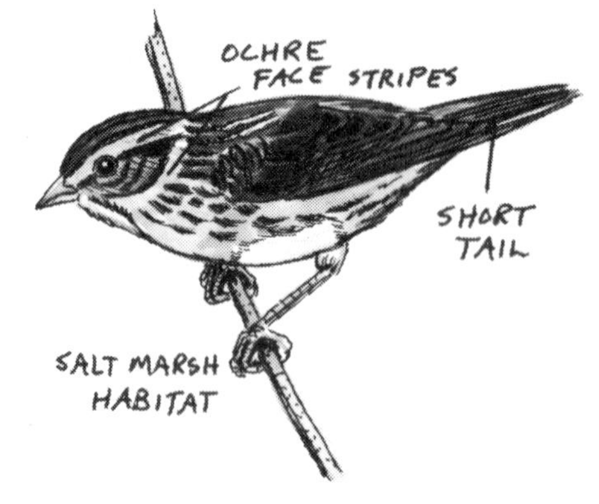

Song Sparrow

5-7'' (year round)

Our most common sparrow. Sings from bush tops. Heavily streaked breast with center spot and long tail helps to identify this widespread sparrow. Song starts with two or three notes, then continues with a short melody.

White-throated Sparrow

6-7'' (Sept.-May)

A larger-than-average sparrow of winter months. Bright white throat, gray breast and belly. Light-and-dark-striped crown with a yellow spot between bill and eye help to identify this ground-dwelling, feeder bird.

Dark-eyed Junco

6'' (Oct.-April)

This is our gray-and-white snowbird. Gray above; white belly and white outer tail feathers which flash when in flight. A ground-dwelling bird, common at bird feeders.

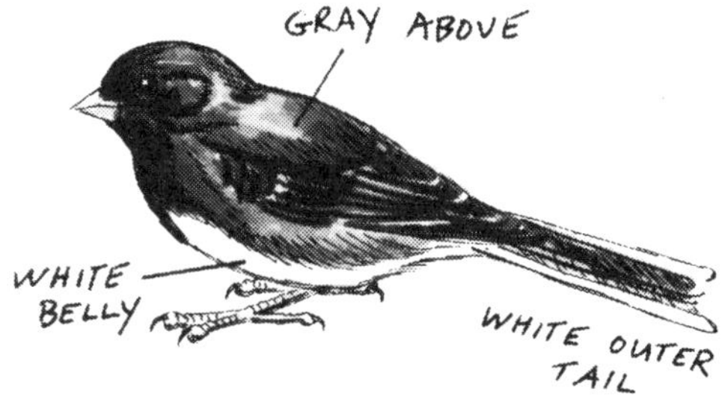

Blackbirds

Three species of blackbirds occur on the Cape. (The aforementioned Starling is not in the blackbird family.) All blackbirds flock, that is, gather and move in numbers and are fairly easy to separate and identify, although the females can be confusing to beginners.

Red-winged Blackbird

7-10'' (March-Nov.)

Our common marsh blackbird. Black overall with orange/red shoulder patches trimmed in yellow. Females look like big, heavily streaked sparrows.

Common Grackle

11-14'' (March-Nov.)

This is the **glossy, long-tailed** blackbird. Iridescent purplish-green on head, neck, and breast. Yellow eyes. Often in large flocks with other blackbirds. Found in all habitats, especially in residential areas.

Brown-headed Cowbird

7'' (April-Oct.)

A small, unfamiliar, yet common and widespread blackbird. Male is glossy black overall but has a chocolate brown head. Most often seen walking on lawns. Female is mostly gray brown overall and nondescript. Cowbirds are parasitic, that is, they lay eggs in other birds' nests and depend on these nesters to rear their young.

Orioles and Finches

Northern Oriole

7-8'' (May-Sept.)

Bright-orange-and-black with white wing bars. Black head and wings; orange breast and belly. Tail is black with orange outer edges. Female is drab overall. Nests high in trees; sings rich, musical notes from treetops.

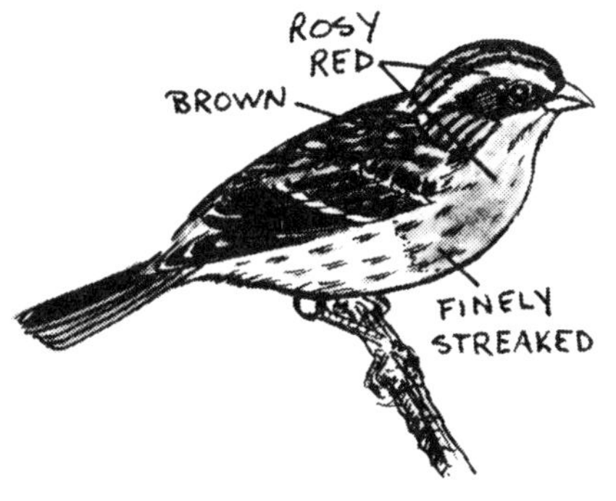

House Finch

5-6'' (year round, abundant)

This is the bird that everyone mistakenly calls Purple Finch. It is **not** the Purple Finch which has become scarce on Cape Cod. Virtually all rosy red finches are **House** Finches. House Finches are common at feeders and nest in houseplants, porch lights, signs, and so forth. Males show rosy red of varying degrees, depending on age. Females are brown and finely streaked.

American Goldfinch

5'' (year round)

Very common. This yellow, black, and white finch fools a lot of people. Adult male in breeding plumage is easy to identify—black cap, black wings, and black tail with bright yellow throat, breast, back, and belly. At feeders, any olive green, yellowish finch with **two white** wing bars is a goldfinch in **non-breeding** plumage. This ''wild canary'' sings as it flies in a deeply undulating pattern.

House Sparrow

6'' (year round)

Preferred habitat is residential neighborhoods and fast-food-restaurant parking lots. Male has a black bib and gray crown. Female is brown with white eye stripe. This is not a sparrow, but actually a Eurasian weaver finch introduced to the United States in the late nineteenth century.

Birding Tour No. 1

Birds of the Woodlands, Spring and Summer

One of the most exciting times to watch birds is during their spring migration. Most birds are in their breeding plumage, the weather is pleasantly warm, and the birds often move through in waves providing great opportunities to look at numbers of birds. Birds, such as warblers, vireos, sparrows, swallows, and finches, are active, brightly colored and sing jubilantly in the spring. A number of these species nests on the Cape and can be observed through the month of July and even into August.

Almost any pine-oak forest will produce birds, but a few areas stand out as birding hot-spots. The Lowell Holly Reservation in Mashpee, the Wellfleet Bay Wildlife Sanctuary in Wellfleet, and the Beech Forest in Provincetown are areas that provide food, shelter, and water for spring migrants and nesting species. Look and listen for birds high and low. You may not be able to identify a bird by its song at first; but, once you see a warbler or sparrow throw its head back, point its beak to the sky, and let go a chorus, you will be able to associate that bird with its song forever.

Three common species of woodland warblers are the Black-and-white Warbler, the Pine Warbler and the Ovenbird. The Black-and-white Warbler is vivid and boldly patterned; the Pine Warbler and the Ovenbird are fairly drab and seldom seen, yet their songs ring out over the woodland. Although you will hear the Pine Warbler sing its monotone trill from high up in the pitch pines, finding this little pale yellow warbler may not be easy. The Ovenbird is a hard-to-find resident of the forest floor. Its song, steadily rising in volume, sounds like *teacher, teacher, teacher, teacher, teacher.* Just when you think you've walked close enough to see it, the song will start up behind you! Another secretive bird, the Red-eyed Vireo, spends its days in treetops, and sings short, musical phrases over and over again. Several species of birds that have visited feeders over the winter months also occupy the woodlands in spring. The Tufted Titmouse, Black-capped Chickadee, White-breasted Nuthatch, and Downy Woodpecker all nest on the Cape.

Along the woodland edge listen for the

bubbly, gurgling phrases of the Gray Catbird. This mimic, which is gray with a black cap, is familiar in yards and gardens. The brilliant Yellow Warbler is found along all edge habitats, especially near water. The hard-to-see but very vocal Common Yellowthroat sings *wichity wichity wichity,* always close to the ground, in dense undergrowth. This tiny warbler, greenish with a bright yellow throat and black face mask, nests over the entire Cape. When the woodland borders a pond or lake, a greater variety of birds may be found. The Eastern Phoebe is a flycatcher, as is the Eastern Kingbird. Both sit on bare branches over or near water; they flit off to catch an insect and then return to perch. The phoebe is olive-green/gray above (with no wing bars), and is pale below. It has a distinct habit of pumping its tail up and down. The call is a nasal *fee-bee*. The Eastern Kingbird is unmistakable; it is jet black above and pure white below with a white band at the tip of the tail. Look also for swallows skimming over the surface of the pond. Both the Tree Swallow and the Barn Swallow eat thousands of mosquitoes and other flying insects each day. The brilliant blue back of the Tree Swallow and the deeply forked tail of the Barn Swallow are field marks that confirm identification of these fast-flying insect eaters.

In woodland meadows or adjacent fields, especially where Eastern Red Cedar or Pitch Pine are prevalent, look and listen for the Prairie Warbler. This tiny warbler is often heard before it is seen. Listen for a rapid series of notes rising in pitch. Another bird that sings from bushtops is the Song Sparrow. This is the common sparrow of the Cape and is found everywhere. It is brown above and pale below; it has heavy brown streaks on the breast which form a center spot. Song Sparrow territories overlap throughout yards, meadows, and wood edges. Not as numerous but nesting and living close to the ground in the Scrub Oak thickets is the Rufous-sided Towhee. Towhees rustle the leaves with a two-footed shuffle as they look for insects and grubs, the insects' larvae. Towhees give two distinct songs: *chew-wink* and *drink-your-teee.* Either call will give away the presence of this secretive black, white, and chestnut-colored relative of the sparrow.

Songbirds are everywhere during May and June! On some days, when all conditions are perfect for migration, the numbers of birds and their variety may seem overwhelming to both the casual and experienced bird-watcher. Remember, take your time. Look at every bird. You'll get better every time out!

Birding Tour No. 2

Waterfowl of Freshwater Lakes and Ponds

The great variety of lakes, ponds, and marshes on the Cape provides shelter and food for many species of ducks and other waterfowl. Shallow, vegetated ponds and creeks attract dabbling ducks, Canada Geese, and the Mute Swan, while the deeper ponds attract the diving ducks. Any season will provide the birding enthusiast with good views of ducks, but generally, fall, winter, and spring are best for observing numbers of species. Although a diversity of duck species is present in summer, most ducks are rather rare at this season and tend to be secretive as nesting is under way. Also, most have molted into a dull brown non-breeding, or eclipse, plumage and remain this way until the fall when they take on the breeding plumage of the upcoming spring.

It is during November through April that we see the best variety and the greatest number of freshwater ducks on the Cape and Islands. Several ponds stand out as hot-spots, predictable sources for waterfowl viewing. They are Siders Pond and Salt Pond in the center of Falmouth; Hallets Mill Pond, off Route 6A in Cummaquid, Barnstable; Lovers Lake in Chatham; Great Pond and Herring Pond in Eastham; and Cliff Pond in Nickerson State Park, Brewster. These ponds will usually have several species present and, in combination, could provide many of the freshwater species possible on the Cape. A number of species, especially the diving ducks and mergansers, may appear in saltwater estuaries or tidal creeks, especially when ponds and lakes are frozen.

The two most common ducks to be found on the Cape and Islands are the Mallard (easily identified by its green head, white neck ring, rusty breast, and yellow bill), and the Black Duck (actually very dark brown with a paler brown head and with a dull, mustard yellow bill). The two are often together and do interbreed. The female Mallard is brown overall, lighter than the Black Duck, and has an orange bill. The Mallard is an introduced species and may ultimately cause the extinction of the pure Black Duck through interbreeding. A stately looking duck is the Northern Pintail, named for its long black tail feathers. The Pintail's chocolate brown head contrasts with its white neck and breast; a single white stripe extends up the side of the head. Females are light brown overall and may be identified by their noticeably long, thin neck. Another handsome duck is the American Wigeon. A gray head with green stripe through the eye and a white cap and forehead help to identify this handsome drake (male). Females are brown with a gray head and rusty sides. All of these ducks are dabblers—they feed in shallow water by tipping up to reach vegetation.

Two more dabbler species, very small in comparison to the others, are the Blue-winged Teal and Green-winged Teal. Both are easily identified by their head pattern and small size. The Green-winged Teal, the more common of the two, is the smallest dabbler and has a chestnut-colored head with a green ear patch bordered in white. The Blue-winged Teal has a bluish gray head with a striking white crescent between the bill and the eye. The females of both species are small and brown. Think of the **name** of the species as you notice the green or blue wing patches. It will help you identify the female teals. Two species of dabbling ducks that are less common but should be looked for are the Gadwall and the Northern Shoveler. The Gadwall may be hard to identify because of its non-descript coloration. The male appears mostly gray, but look for the black tail area and the small white patch on the wing. Females resemble female Mallards but have the white wing patch. A good spot to find Gadwalls during the winter is Mill Pond at the intersection of Routes 149 and 28 in Marstons Mills, Barnstable. The shoveler's huge, spatulate bill and chestnut, green, and white plumage should help to identify this uncommon duck. Two species of large waterfowl occur on freshwater ponds, the Canada Goose and the Mute Swan (an introduced species).

Of the diving ducks found in freshwater ponds and lakes, the Bufflehead is the most common. Equally at home in fresh or salt water, this small diver often forms large flocks and is widespread. The Ring-necked Duck and the two species of scaup are also common diving ducks. The Greater Scaup and Lesser Scaup are so difficult to separate in the field that even experts simply refer to them as scaup species. Both are dark-fronted with white sides and gray backs. Females appear brown overall with a broad white patch at the base of the bill. The Ring-necked Duck has the same overall pattern as the scaup but has a white ring close to the bill tip and has a noticeable white flash between the breast and sides. Look also for the small Ruddy Duck with its white cheeks, dark cap, and characteristically cocked tail. Two uncommon diving ducks are the Canvasback and the Redhead. Both have a chestnut head, black breast, and grayish sides but are easily separated by head profile: the Canvasback has a long, sloping forehead and beak.

Two species of waterfowl often encountered in fresh water that are not in the duck family are the Pied-billed Grebe and the American Coot. Both are easy to identify. The Pied-billed Grebe is brown and tiny, smaller even than the Bufflehead; it has a stout, pointed bill. Often seen near pond edges, the little "hell-diver" can disappear beneath the surface without a ripple. The coot is dark gray overall with a distinct, white bill. It feeds both by dabbling and diving.

Nineteen species of freshwater ducks and waterfowl are mentioned here. This may seem like a lot, but by watching and separating the dabblers from the divers, the choices are narrowed considerably. Any of these species may be encountered by visiting the ponds mentioned above, so take your time and have fun!

Birding Tour No. 3

Common Birds of the Salt Marsh

Around much of the perimeter of Cape Cod is a fringe of green. This area, situated behind the protective dunes and at the foot of the gently sloping upland, is one of calm, open, and often expansive and wet grassland. This is the salt marsh. Influenced by every tide, it is rich in life and in life-giving nutrients. Salt marshes of Cape Cod may be huge, such as the marsh in Barnstable and the marsh at West Dennis Beach. Others may only be small patches of the marsh grass Spartina.

During any season, birds can be found in the salt marsh. In some cases, it's possible to walk in the marsh; in others, it is better to scan the marsh with binoculars or spotting scope to find its avian inhabitants. Winter is the quietest season. The period between May and October will produce the greatest number and variety of birds, both nesting species and migrants.

The salt marsh in winter appears brown, bleak, cold, and wind-blown. It **is** all of these. Only the hardiest birds occur in its flooded creeks. Most common of these is the Black Duck. A solid-colored, dark brown dabbler or puddle duck, it is virtually the only dabbler found abundantly in salt water. Canada Geese flock in the marsh to feed, as well as roost, both in the high marsh and along its watery edge. Along the creek edges a long-legged Great Blue Heron may linger, while two species of diving ducks, the Red-breasted Merganser and the Bufflehead, chase the same mummichogs hunted stealthily by the wading heron. The merganser, which also frequents the open seas, is easily identified by its dark green head, white neck ring, and conspicuous crest. Females have the same crested shape, but appear reddish-brown overall. The Bufflehead, a small duck, is black and white. Most obvious on the male is a bold white head patch over most of the crown. The female is dark overall with a small white patch behind the eye. Look for the Northern Harrier (or Marsh Hawk) low over the salt marsh as it courses to hunt for ducks, or look along the marsh edges as it searches for its favorite prey, the Meadow Vole. The white rump patch immediately identifies this long-winged hawk.

During April and May a steady stream of migrants arrives at the salt marsh. First to be seen and heard is the Red-winged Blackbird. Bright red-and-yellow shoulder patches identify this blackbird, which will nest and remain until fall. The Laughing Gull is our only black-headed gull. This loud, crow-sized gull feeds and nests in the high marsh. Throughout the warm months, look for the Snowy Egret. Widespread in the Cape's salt marshes, this is the white egret of the marsh. Black bill, black legs, and yellow feet help to identify it. Another heron, small and dark, stands motionless at the edge of the marsh—the Green-backed Heron. Anyone who is in the vicinity of a salt marsh at dusk or after dark may hear the call of Black-crowned Night Herons. These stocky herons, gray and white, with a black cap, call *kwok* as they fly overhead, often in twos and threes as they leave their daytime roost to forage in the marsh at night. Some birds may be difficult to observe in the tall marsh grass. The Willet (a large sandpiper) and the Sharp-tailed Sparrow may be seen flying over the salt marsh and may be identified readily by their behavior. Both birds nest in the salt marsh. The Willet calls a loud *wi-wi-llet, wi-wi-llet, wi-wi-llet* incessantly as it swoops past any intruder on the marsh and flashes its bright white wing patches. The tiny Sharp-tailed Sparrow is more subtle. Its ochre-colored face patch is not easily seen as it quickly jumps from the grass, flies along 15-20 feet at grass height, then drops, and disappears. The jump-and-drop behavior of this very secretive sparrow helps to identify it. All through the warm months, swallows zigzag over the marsh to catch insects on the wing. Tree Swallows and Barn Swallows are most common.

Common Terns and Least Terns hover over marsh creeks and dive for mummichogs. Although these two gray-and-white, black-capped seabirds are seen more commonly along the seashore, they often follow the rising tide into the salt marsh. Another bird that hovers and dives for fish is the Belted Kingfisher. Usually before the Kingfisher is seen, its long, rattling call echoes across the marsh. This crested, blue-and-white fisher perches nearby at the water's edge.

As the nesting season wanes, fall migrants begin to appear along the Cape's shoreline. Most of these are shorebirds—sandpipers and plovers. A few, most notably the tiny Least Sandpiper, prefer the muddy creek edges of the salt marsh. Willets, though still in the marsh, are much less noisy with no nest to protect. Small flocks of Greater Yellowlegs stand in shallow water. Snowy Egrets, often in sizable flocks, prepare to head south. Flocks of Black-bellied Plovers often rest in the marsh while the larger Whimbrel, with its striped head and strongly decurved bill, forages for Fiddler Crabs and plucks them from their burrows.

All of Cape Cod's habitats support bird populations. By visiting certain habitats, we often encounter predictable bird species. The salt marsh is one of the many habitats where the bird-watcher can predict, find, and identify species easily. So get out there with binoculars and find all the species mentioned here. They're all there and waiting.

Birding Tour No. 4

Shorebirds of the Tidal Flats in late Summer

It's late summer, a time when shorebirds are at the peak of their southward migration over Cape Cod. These birds have completed their nesting season in the far north and are making their way to the southern United States and South America for the winter. They begin to appear along our shores in early July; although some may linger into the winter months, most will have headed south over the Atlantic by late September.

The term **shorebirds** is the collective name for sandpipers, plovers, oystercatchers, and their allies. A good variety is here in late August—it is easier than you may think to sort them out and identify them. Find the American Oyster-catchers first. They stand out from all other birds because of their size and bright orange bill. One of the largest shorebirds, these black, brown, and white shellfish eaters are often found on the mussel beds. Two other large shorebirds of the tidal flats are the Willet and the Greater Yellowlegs. Both are sandpipers. In flight, the Willet is unmistakable with its large, flashy white wing patches. At rest this gray, nondescript shorebird with dull gray legs stands almost as tall as the oystercatchers. Listen for the Willet's call—a loud *wi-wi-llet, wi-wi-llet*—repeated again and again. The Greater Yellowlegs stands almost as tall as the Willet, but it appears more slender and has bright yellow legs, an unmistakable field mark. Both the Willet and the Greater Yellowlegs have a relatively long bill and long legs. Not as common, the Lesser Yellowlegs is nearly identical in plumage to the Greater, but it is smaller, with a thin, petite bill. The majority of yellowlegs seen are Greater Yellowlegs, but it's worth taking a second look. Next, look for a shorter, chunky sandpiper with a very long bill. Its reddish brown plumage and bold white eye stripe identify it as a Short-billed Dowitcher. True, this bird has a very long bill, but it is not the rare Long-billed Dowitcher, which prefers non-tidal habitats. All dowitchers show a white flash up the middle of the back in flight; look for it.

Two types of plovers are probably here, the Semipalmated Plover and the Black-bellied Plover. The Semipalmated Plover is small, brown above and white below, and has a dark ring around its neck. They may be here in large numbers. So may the black-belly. If it is in breeding plumage, it is easy to identify: black below, white on the sides of its neck and breast, and mottled black and white on its back. Remember, though, that in non-breeding plumage it is a nondescript, mottled brown and white. Now find the Ruddy Turnstone, the calico cat of the bird world. This rusty brown, black, and white bird with orange legs looks like a cross between a sandpiper and a plover. The last of the robin-sized birds to be found on these tidal flats is the Red Knot. It is gray on the back, brick red (bright or dull) below, and has short legs and a short bill. Although you may often find knots in groups feeding with dowitchers, you should not confuse the two species if you note the obvious differences in bill length.

Now focus your binoculars on the smallest sandpipers. Three sparrow-sized species may be found. The Sanderling is the largest of these and appears in a variety of plumages, depending on its sex and age. In spring through late summer, the Sanderling appears chestnut (bright or dull) above and white below. Later in the season the Sanderling molts to a pearly gray above and white below. The bill is rather short and black. The Semipalmated Sandpiper is probably the most abundant of all the shorebirds observed. It is small, dull, brownish gray above and streaked and pale below, with a black bill. They seem to run around everywhere. The Least Sandpiper is tiny. Best identified by its smallest size and pale, drab yellow legs, leasties are usually found near the grassy edges of the tidal flats.

There! You've made it through the most common shorebirds found on the Cape and Islands! Almost any tidal flats from Provincetown to Martha's Vineyard will offer a variety of migrant shorebirds. Be patient, sort them out, have fun!

Birding Tour No. 5

Fall and Winter Migrants on Salt Water

In late autumn, when cold winds blow hard from the northwest, up to twenty-five species of ducks can be seen in Cape Cod waters. Some duck species occur primarily on the open seas, some prefer saltwater bays and rivers, and others prefer the habitat of freshwater ponds and lakes.

Let us first visit the open waters of Cape Cod Bay. Many locations on the bay will provide good views of wintering and migrating ducks, as well as views of loons, grebes, gulls, and gannets. Three of the choicest locations are Sandy Neck Beach in Barnstable, Corporation Beach in Dennis, and First Encounter Beach in Eastham. All these places provide an opportunity to view the open water from your parked car. To see some birds that may be well offshore, it is helpful to use a spotting scope.

All sea ducks dive beneath the surface to feed on fish or mollusks. Look first for the Common Eider. This is a black-and-white duck; in fact, it is the biggest duck you will see. Often seen in floating flocks, called rafts, the black-capped, white-faced males are accompanied by the chestnut brown females and mottled brown-and-white immature males. In flight, eider (like most sea ducks) fly low over the water in wavy lines. Three species of scoters may be seen on the winter seas. The males are all quite distinctive. The Black Scoter, smallest of the three, is all-black with an orange knob on the bill. The Surf Scoter is also black but shows a white patch on the forehead and nape, hence the nickname skunkhead. The third and largest scoter is the White-winged Scoter; it is all-black but for a white comma-shaped patch over the eye and a white wing patch visible on the side as it swims. Females of all three species are a dull brown and can be difficult to identify at a distance. Female Black Scoters show a pale cheek and throat contrasting with a darker cap. Female Surf Scoters may show dull white face patches. The female White-winged Scoter also shows dull face patches and may show a white wing patch when swimming. If any scoter shows a white wing patch, it is a White-winged Scoter. All three species of scoters and the Common Eider often form rafts of hundreds, or even thousands, of birds.

So, the appearance of large numbers does not necessarily mean a great variety of species.

Another very widespread, often numerous duck is the Red-breasted Merganser. Separate this species from the previous four by its long-necked, streamlined shape, especially in flight. Males have a dark green crested head and broad white neck ring. Females are reddish brown on the crest, head, and neck. Both sexes show prominent white wing patches. Bufflehead and Common Goldeneye have wing patches also, but are chunky and smaller and show white face patches. They are found in the open waters of Cape Cod Bay only during migration. Keep an eye out for the brown-winged, white-bodied Oldsquaw to dart by. This small sea duck has a distinctive brown band across its white breast.

Two species of loons may be encountered. Look for the Common Loon, which is blackish above, with a white cheek, throat and breast. Also note the dagger-like bill. The Common Loon is larger than the largest ducks. The Red-throated Loon is smaller and grayer than the Common Loon with a thin pointed bill that appears upturned. Remembering that loons occur singly will help you separate them from ducks. The Horned Grebe, a loonlike bird of the open seas, has the same dark-above/white-below pattern and is usually solitary. But, it is very small and square-headed.

During the winter months a bird often found in the grassy beach edges of the bay is the Brant, a stocky, black-necked goose. Compared to the Canada Goose, the other possibility, the Brant is smaller, lacks a white cheek, and is black on the breast (the Canada Goose has a pale breast).

Gulls may be observed constantly. Our common gray Herring Gull and the larger Great Black-backed Gull are ever present and may be observed year round. In late November, look for the tiny Bonaparte's Gull flying by. Only half the size of the Herring Gull and often appearing in small flocks, this gray-and-white gull shows a distinctive white flash at the end of the wing, a petite black bill, and a black spot behind the eye.

Northern Gannets may be observed on some days, especially when there are north or northeast winds. Adult gannets are pure white with black outer wings. Juvenile and immature birds are dark brown or mottled brown and white, but are the size of the adults. Gannets are very big, larger than any gull, and appear pointed at the head, tail and wings. They dive like rockets into the sea to feed on fish and squid.

Although the variety of species is often low in Cape Cod Bay during the winter, with only a few species represented, the bay will often be teeming with several thousand birds. Look at them all and sort them out. Have fun!

Birding Tour No. 6

Oceanic Birds

Almost any visitor to Cape Cod who has an interest in nature eventually goes on a whale watch. Good-sized, comfortable boats leave from Plymouth, Barnstable, and Provincetown every day in summer for the same destination, an underwater mound north of Provincetown called Stellwagen Bank. Here, a rapid change in sea depth, water temperature, and salinity brings about a great diversity of marine organisms—from microscopic plankton to the massive whales which are its primary consumers. On such a sea trip, the amateur naturalist and bird-watcher are also given the opportunity to observe some of the most fascinating avian life on our planet, the free-roaming pelagic seabirds, most notably shearwaters and storm-petrels. Most of these seabirds which are seen by us during our summer (but actually their winter) are thousands of miles from the islands in the South Atlantic and Antarctic regions where they nest. On some days, shearwaters and storm-petrels may occur in the thousands, while on other days they are absent altogether.

Only one species of storm-petrel is normally observed on whale watches; this is the Wilson's Storm-petrel. The other possibility, the Leach's Storm-petrel, is very rarely seen on Stellwagen Bank. Wilson's is the storm-petrel that we commonly see offshore. Three species of shearwaters—the Greater Shearwater, the Sooty Shearwater, and the less common Manx Shearwater—are all a pretty good bet during the late summer and fall.

As you leave the harbor, whether it be Plymouth, Barnstable, or Provincetown, look for Double-crested Cormorants on rocks or pilings. These upright-standing black birds with orange bills are often observed with wings spread as they stand in the sun. The Herring Gull, our common gray-and-white seagull, is everywhere, as is the larger, but less numerous, Great Black-backed Gull. Immatures of both species are a mottled brown and remain so for two and three years respectively. If you head north out over the open water toward Stellwagen Bank, you will see numbers of terns. These are almost certainly all Common Terns, but the Roseate Tern, now federally endangered, may occur. The two species are more easily identified by call although they differ slightly in color. The calls are quite different. Listen for the nasal *chi-vik, chi-vik, chi-vik* of the Roseate Tern and the Common Tern's harsh *kee-eer kee-eer* call. Listen carefully—you might find a roseate or two. Both are graceful, fork-tailed, gray-and-white seabirds with long pointed wings and a black cap. Roseates are more silvery on the upper parts and have long, streaming, white tail feathers. The Common Tern is grayer and has a forked tail with black on the outer edges. The Least Tern is much smaller than either the Common or Roseate Tern. Most notable is its short tail and tiny size. The call is a high-pitched, squeaky *ki-dik ki-dee, ki-dik ki-dee.* Least Terns, like the common and roseates, hover and dive for fish all day long. Look for these birds as you leave or enter harbors.

Most people on the boat are looking for spouts. Suddenly a small, black bird flies past the bow, close to the water—a Wilson's Storm-petrel. This bird is all black, is about the size of a cardinal, and has a white rump patch. Wilson's Storm-petrels patter over the surface when they feed. Keep watch for the Sooty Shearwater and Greater Shearwater, crow-sized birds with long, stiff wings. The Sooty Shearwater is unmistakable; it is a dark chocolate brown all over, with silvery underwings. The Greater Shearwater is a bit larger; it is brown above and has a dark black cap, a pale collar, a white breast, and a white rump patch. You might also notice the brown belly smudge. Both shearwaters fly fast and alternate several flaps with a water-shearing glide. A smaller shearwater is the Manx Shearwater, less common (usually) than the two previous species and almost half their size. Manx Shearwaters have no white rump patch and are dark brown (almost black) above and pure white below. They have the same shape and characteristics as the other shearwaters, but the Manx is smaller and usually solitary. Look also for the Parasitic Jaeger (yay,ger). It is gull-like and dark brown above with creamy pale undersides. The mark to look for is the white flash near the tip of each wing. Jaegers are kleptoparasites, that is, they live by stealing food, most often from terns. So watch for the chase—one of the birds may be a jaeger—but do not be confused by immature Laughing Gulls, which are very common offshore. One other pelagic bird to look for, which is a special treat to observe, is the rare Northern Fulmar. This bird (not mentioned earlier) has the same color pattern as the Herring Gull (white head and underparts with a pale gray back and upper wings) but differs in shape and flight. Fulmars look like a stocky shearwater and fly with stiff wings and a rapid wingbeat. They're tough to find but don't count them out!

Whale-watching trips provide an excellent opportunity to see oceanic birds that are rarely seen otherwise. The ocean is a big place with lots of room, so don't be discouraged if you see very few birds. Sometimes you will see thousands of birds; sometimes, none. In late summer or fall, it's tough to miss seeing some birds. Remember, look at every bird and have fun!

Index

Cape Cod Museum of Natural History Publications

The Flora of Cape Cod: An Annotated List of the Ferns and Flowering Plants of Barnstable County, Massachusetts, by Dr. Henry K. Svenson and Dr. Robert W. Pyle. 1979. 139 pp. $6.95

A Guide to the Common Birds of Cape Cod by Peter Trull. 1991. 72 pp. $8.95.

Natural History Series

No. 1. *The Evergreens of Cape Cod*
by Donald Schall. 1982. 12 pp. $1.50

No. 2. *Marine Mollusks of Cape Cod*
by Donald J. Zinn. 1984. 80 pp. $6.95

No. 3. *Crabs of Cape Cod*
by Stephan Berrick. 1986. 80 pp. $6.95

No. 4. *Dragonflies and Damselflies of Cape Cod* by Virginia Carpenter. 1991. 80 pp., 8 color plates. $9.95

Conservation Leaflet Series

The Alewife	$ .50
The Box Turtle	$ .50
Least Terns	$ .50
The Living Fossil (Horseshoe Crab)	$ .50
The Piping Plover	$ .50
Sea Lavender	$ .50
The Short-Eared Owl	$ .50

The above publications are available from The Cape Cod Museum of Natural History, Box 1710, Brewster, Massachusetts, 02631. Please add 50¢ for postage and handling for each Conservation Leaflet order of one or more, $1.50 for other publications.

The Cape Cod Museum of Natural History is a nonprofit education, research and interpretive center founded in 1954 and focused on the natural environment of Cape Cod. Our mission is to inspire and promote a better understanding and appreciation of the environment and the means to sustain it. Membership is open to individuals, families and organizations. Members receive free admission to the Museum, six newletters about Museum activities yearly, use of its facilities, reduced rates on classes, programs, special trips and exhibits, discounts in the Museum shop, library borrowing privileges, and The Cape Naturalist, the Museum's environmental journal.

Membership categories include:

Family $35
Individual $25
Student* $5

*Away from home; not eligible for reduced program rates.

Contributions are deductible for Income Tax purposes. Checks may be made payable to The Cape Cod Museum of Natural History, Inc., Box 1710, Brewster, Massachusetts 02631.